Urban
Housing
Strategies

Urban Housing Strategies

Education and Realization

Patrick I. Wakely
Hartmut Schmetzer
Babar K. Mumtaz

Foreword by
Otto H. Koenigsberger

PITMAN PUBLISHING

First published 1976

Pitman Publishing Ltd
Pitman House, Parker Street, Kingsway, London WC2B 5PB
PO Box 46038, Banda Street, Nairobi, Kenya

Pitman Publishing Pty Ltd
Pitman House, 158 Bouverie Street, Carlton, Victoria 3053, Australia

Pitman Publishing Corporation
6 East 43 Street, New York, NY 10017, USA

Sir Isaac Pitman (Canada) Ltd
495 Wellington Street West, Toronto 135, Canada

The Copp Clark Publishing Company
517 Wellington Street West, Toronto 135, Canada

ISBN 273 00445 X

Text set in 12/13 pt Photon Univers at the Pitman Press,
Bath. Printed and bound by Knapp, Drewett and Sons Ltd,
Kingston upon Thames. (1920 : 73).

CONTENTS

Role of project work
Project as generator of needs
Role of the teacher
Teaching traditional solutions
Products and processes
Selection of projects
Groupwork
Division of labour

FOREWORD

The *Development Planning Unit* exists to help developing countries solve the problems of their fast growing cities. Its first concern is the creation of the professional cadres needed for this purpose.

It started by offering post-experience courses to architects, planners, engineers and social scientists engaged in urban development work. To reach larger numbers, this service was extended to cover training facilities for teachers in these professions and mid-career courses for senior practitioners and urban administrators. Special relationships were established with faculties of planning and architecture in developing countries to facilitate exchanges of students and teachers and assist in the development of new courses and research programmes.

In 1972, an *Extension Service* for schools of Architecture and Planning was added to the list of these facilities. Teams of teachers from the Development Planning Unit visit overseas universities and professional schools at their invitation to co-operate with their opposite numbers and groups of students in the study of urban development problems. This book is based on the first three years experience of the Extension Service.

This period must be looked upon as an experiment in teaching—or rather in joint learning. The purpose of the Extension Service visits is to stimulate innovation in the host schools and to foster the self-confidence which teachers, students and practitioners in developing countries need to cope with problems for which no textbook solutions or Western precedents exist. The visits must be short (six to eight weeks) and the courses well-prepared to make the best use of the short time available. Each course must be planned for the special needs of a different school and city. During the initial three years the subject was always 'Housing'; the teaching was always informal and project-based with emphasis on the understanding of user needs and on the search for policies or strategies rather than the design of buildings. The chapters describing the working methods, the identification of housing stress, the surveys of client groups, the brain-storming sessions and the emerging strategies in their surprising variety convey some of the excitement that the participants must have felt during these visits.

It is perhaps too early to evaluate the experiment. There are encouraging signs, such as students who were stimulated to embark on projects of their own and requests from universities for return visits, additional teaching material and help to incorporate the subject matter of the visits into normal curricula; enough to justify the continuation of the Extension Service. Enquiries and bookings for the second three years period are coming in steadily not only from university schools of architecture, but also from government and city departments of planning and housing and administrative training institutes.

Such requests are essential if the Extension Service is to be run and financed as a technical assistance operation. During the first three years this was not possible because the service was in its infancy and largely unknown. It could not have started without the help of the Nuffield Foundation which paid the visiting teams' salaries during this critical period. It is fitting that the account of the Extension Service should begin with thanks to the Foundation. The Director and Trustees had the vision to recognize the potential of the idea and the courage of backing it at a time when it was no more than an idea of an enthusiastic team of young teachers.

Development Planning Unit,
School of Environmental Studies,
University College, London.
November 1975

OTTO H. KOENIGSBERGER

INTRODUCTION

Urban Housing Strategies is divided into two parts. The first is intended to construct the argument and present the case for basing the training of professionals on a process of enquiry into the nature of problems that have no precedent; in particular problems of human settlement. The second part is presented as a manual of techniques or exercises that have proved useful in getting to grips with the major issues of urban housing and the search for their solution. Though each paper in Part 2 is presented as an independent technique to be studied when needed, they support and exemplify the procedures outlined in the first part.

Part 1 opens with two chapters setting the context in which an approach to housing and learning has been developed. The issues of urban housing are rapidly becoming common knowledge and yet the problems, outlined in the first chapter remain a challenge to city administrations and their professional staff. In this section it is suggested that, by approaching such problems with a rigorous method of enquiry and evaluation, a better understanding of the issues will direct the search for solutions. This argument is expanded in chapter 3 by outlining an approach to the understanding of the dominant features of the supply and demand for urban housing. The chapter concludes by pointing out the changes in professional attitude involved in this approach. Enquiry can be a didactic process and lends itself as well to training as to practice. Chapter 4 contains the theoretical development of the idea which is elaborated in chapter 5 by describing an educational experiment based on the concepts outlined in the first four chapters. The observations made here are drawn directly from the authors' experience of running courses in several schools of planning and architecture.

In 1972 they were given resources to assemble technical material and to develop teaching methods for a series of intensive project-based courses on the economic, social, managerial and technical issues of urban housing. The courses had to be flexible enough to respond to the varied backgrounds and qualifications of different participants and the problems and potentials of different cities. At the same time, the courses had to be sufficiently structured to raise the fundamental issues of urban housing and appropriate methods of arriving at solutions. Subsequently the course has been run with the students and staff of schools of architecture and planning in seven different cities in Asia and Africa. Courses were held at the request of various institutions not only as an experiment in intensive teaching but also as demonstrations of project-based learning, using real situations, with all their complexities.

The approach to urban housing expounded in the course as well as in the chapters that follow has drawn heavily on the teaching of Otto Koenigsberger, whose concept of Action Planning* stands as one of the most significant contributions to the changing of attitudes towards the planning and management of rapidly growing cities. The writings of Charles Abrams† and John F. C. Turner‡ have focused the authors' attention on the essential role of the users of housing in the production of dwellings and on the problems of the management of housing. The approach to design and problem solving was largely influenced by the work of J. Christopher Jones§, the publications of the conferences on design methods held in England, in the 1960s¶, and by Michael Lloyd's pedagogic reforms in Ghana and at the Architectural Association School in London. It has been developed or modified as a result of working with many different students and teachers of the following:

Academy of Architecture, Bombay
Chandigarh College of Architecture
Department of Architecture, University of Baghdad
Human Settlements Programme, Asian Institute of Technology, Bangkok
Department of Planning, University of Nairobi
Centre for Environmental Planning and Technology, Ahmedabad
Department of Architecture, National College of Art, Lahore
School of Architecture, Hull College of Art.

Much of our understanding of design and teaching methods was inspired by Mario Novella who helped us to conceive the educational experiment and was with us during the initial periods of preparation and the first courses. Anil Nagrath, Geoffrey Taunton, and Neelkanth Chhaya, joined the team for one or several courses and contributed to thinking and practice. We owe a great deal to the continuous and stimulating discussions with our friends and colleagues in the Development Planning Unit.

P.I.W.
H.S.
B.K.M.

* KOENIGSBERGER, O. H., Action Planning, *Architectural Association Journal*, London, May 1964.

† ABRAMS, C., *Housing in the Modern World*, Faber and Faber, London 1966.

‡ TURNER, J. F. C., Housing Priorities, Settlement Patterns and Urban Development in Modernising Countries, *Journal of the American Institute of Planners*, Vol. XXXIV, No. 6, November 1968.

See also *Journal of the American Institute of Planners*, Vol. XXXIII, No. 3, May 1967; *Architectural Design*, London, August 1963.

§ JONES, J. C., *Design Methods: Seeds of Human Futures*, Wiley-Interscience, London 1970.

¶ JONES, J. C. & THORNLEY, D. G. (Eds), *Conference on Design Methods*, Pergamon Press, London 1963. Gregory, F. A. (Ed.), *The Design Method*, Butterworths, London 1966. Broadbent, G. H. & Ward, A. (Eds), *Design Methods in Agriculture*, Lund Humphries, London 1969.

PART 1

HOUSING IN THIRD WORLD CITIES

1

The dominant problem that characterizes the cities of the Third World is the meagre financial resources of the majority of their citizens, and in the public coffers, coupled with unprecedented rates of population growth. A great deal has been written about the 'push factors' which drive peasant farmers to the city from impoverished, overpopulated or unproductive agricultural areas, and about the 'pull factors' of the economic and social alternatives and opportunities offered by urban life that attract people from the countryside*. Rural improvement programmes, family planning campaigns and similar projects are long-term remedies that are unlikely to make a noticeable effect on the rate of growth of urban poverty in the next decade or two. Table 1 lists 20 cities of Africa, Asia and Latin America picked at random and ranked by their population growth rates. They range from Lusaka and Kinshasa, each in the process of doubling their populations every eight years, to Calcutta which is growing at less than one-sixth of the national population growth rate of the whole of India. These rates of increase, expressed as new households per annum and per week in the table are intended to demonstrate orders of magnitude only. No attempt has been made to indicate the number of households already living in temporary shelters, in unserviced slums, in conditions of severe overcrowding or on the streets. And no mention is made of the rate at which the existing housing stock is deteriorating or of the incapacity of urban services.

Most of the cities and towns of the Third World have public sector programmes intended to assist their poorer citizens with their housing; but there are only one or two outstanding exceptions, such as the city-state of Singapore and the colony of Hong Kong, where such programmes have affected the housing conditions of more than a very small minority of the population. The majority, without resources to enter the recognized private housing market, add to the official 'housing deficit'. For example, the Maharashtra Housing Board, responsible for nearly all public housing in Bombay, completed on the average only

---

* BOGUE, D. Internal Migration, in *The Study of Population*, Hauser, P. & Dunkin, O. (Eds), University of Chicago Press, 1959.
  UNITED NATIONS, *The Determinants and Consequences of Population Trends*, ch. 6, Economic and social factors affecting migration.
  MACDONALD, L. & MACDONALD, J. S., Motives and Objectives of Migration: Selective Migration and Preferences toward Rural and Urban Life, *Journal Sociological & Economic Studies*, Vol. 17, No. 4, 1968.
  RICHARDSON, H. W., *Regional Growth Theory*, Macmillan, London 1973.

City	Estimated population 1975 (1)	Annual growth rate % (1)	Population increase per year (1975–76)	Average household size (2)	Increase in households per year	Increase in households per week
Lusaka	435,700	8.9	39,000	4.8	8,100	160
Kinshasa	2,151,300	8.9	191,000	(5)	38,300	740
Bogota	3,610,000	7.2	260,000	5.3	49,000	950
Lagos	1,189,900	6.9	86,000	(5)	17,100	330
Ankara	1,657,100	6.5	108,000	(5)	21,500	410
Santiago, Chile	3,528,900	5.8	205,000	(5)	40,900	790
Nairobi	702,500	5.6	39,000	4.3	9,100	180
Dakar	805,700	5.6	45,000	(5)	9,000	170
Caracas	2,842,600	5.5	156,000	5.8	27,000	520
Baghdad	2,420,900	4.9	119,000	9.0	13,200	250
Jakarta	5,477,900	4.6	252,000	(5)	50,400	970
Mexico City	8,482,900	4.5	382,000	(5)	76,300	1470
Manila	1,561,100	4.3	67,000	(5)	13,400	260
Karachi	3,924,700	4.2	165,000	(5)	33,000	630
Cairo	6,064,900	4.1	249,000	(5)	49,700	960
Bombay	6,903,800	3.7	255,000	5.5	46,400	900
Bangkok	3,654,500	3.5	128,000	6.1	21,000	400
Ahmedabad	1,810,500	3.3	60,000	5.4	11,100	210
Rio de Janeiro	4,857,900	2.7	131,000	(5)	26,200	500
Calcutta	9,200,000	2.3	180,000	(5)	36,000	690

(1) Extrapolated from *Demographic Yearbooks*, United Nations, New York.

(2) Figures (5) are an assumption used for calculation in the absence of data.

(3) Other sources:

LUSAKA, Development Planning Unit—Planned Urban Growth: The Lusaka Experience 1957–73 Mimeo, London 1975.

BANGKOK, Development Planning Unit/Asian Institute of Technology—BKK 75. Mimeo Bangkok 1975.

BOGOTA, Instituto de Credito Teritorial—Vivienda y desarollo Urbano en Colombia, Bogota 1970.

NAIROBI, Nairobi Urban Study Group—Nairobi Metropolitan Growth Strategy, Nairobi City Council, Nairobi 1972.

CARACAS, Direccion General de Estadistica y Censos Nacionales, Estadisticas Annuales, Ministerio de Formento, Caracas 1972.

BAGHDAD, Polservice Masterplan Project—Baghdad Masterplan Vo. 1, Baghdad 1972.

BOMBAY, Development Planning Unit/Academy of Architecture Bombay—Housing in Bombay, Mimeo, Bombay 1973.

AHMEDABAD, Development Planning Unit/Centre for Environmental Planning and Technology AHD 75. Mimeo, Ahmedabad 1975.

CALCUTTA, Kingsley, T. K. & Kristof, F. S.—A housing policy for Metropolitan Calcutta, Ford Foundation, Mimeo, Calcutta 1971. Revised on the basis of 1971 Census figures.

3000 dwelling units per annum in the 17 years between 1948 and 1965* but Table 1 shows that the city is currently growing by 51,000 households every 13 months.

Distribution of resources

The urban agglomerations of the market and mixed economy countries of the Third World are not only characterized by an unprecedented rate of growth but also by a wide disparity in the wealth of their citizens. Figure 1.1 represents the type of income distribution of nearly all the cities under discussion. For instance, in Bombay, which has substantially the highest per capita income of all India's cities, only 5% of the population command earnings of more than £1000 per annum and 40% less than £200 a year*. What is more, as the urban population grows, so does the proportion of the lowest income groups; and this happens without apparently diminishing the power of the wealthy minority. For the sake of simplicity it can be assumed that the increase due to the surplus of births over deaths is evenly distributed over the whole city population, regardless of wealth. But the increase due to migration, which in Caracas accounts for 46% of the city's growth and in Lusaka for over 60%†, goes almost entirely to swelling the ranks of the urban poor with unskilled job seekers from the countryside.

Ability to pay for housing

There is a limited proportion of income that any family can devote to shelter over the other necessities of subsistence, food and clothing. This proportion (rent) directly determines the value of accommodation a household can afford. Thus there exists a straight line relationship between the cost of a dwelling and a household's income (see Fig. 1.2) with the obvious exceptions that the richest households do not have to spend as much as this ratio in providing themselves with suitable housing. Conversely, there is a lower cost threshold below which not even the most modest *acceptable* housing provision can be made on an economic basis. So, households below the 'poverty' line would have to invest increasingly large proportions of their meagre incomes to join the established housing market. But those households whose incomes fall between the 'affluence' and 'poverty lines' can in theory, afford unsubsidized housing. Of course, the size or quality of their homes would be dependent upon their position on the income ladder. However, it is generally only those at the top of the ladder who enjoy the security of regular employment, a sufficiently high income and some collateral that gives them access to credit for the construction of their own dwellings. Hence the private sector housing market is only available to those above the 'credit' line. Those between the 'credit' and 'poverty' lines are denied access to the urban housing market by the rules of financial security and official mistrust. By juxtaposing Figs 1.1 and 1.2 it is apparent that a very large proportion of the urban population fall into this group, though in many cities of the Third World the largest groups are those below the 'poverty' line who cannot enter the recognized market, even in theory.

---

* MAHARASHTRA HOUSING BOARD, Griha Nirman, Vol. 1, Bombay 1966.

* RAMACHANDRAN, P. N., Housing Situation in Greater Bombay, CIDCO Report No. 2, Bombay.

† DIRECCION GENERAL DE ESTADISTICA Y CENSOS NACIONALES, Estadisticas Annuales, Ministerior de Formento, Caracas 1972. Development Planning Unit, Planned Urban Growth: The Lusaka Experience 1957–1973, Mimeo, London 1975.

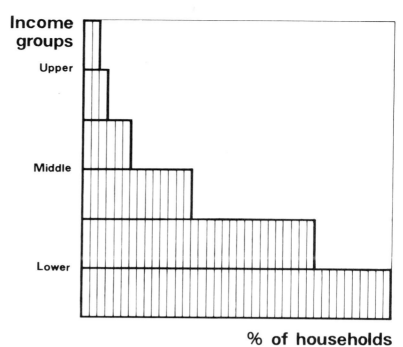

Fig. 1.1

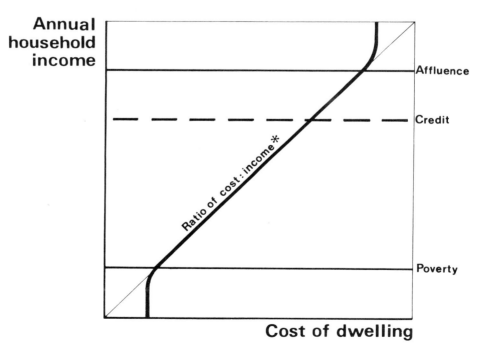

Fig. 1.2 For instance, the UN Economic Commission for Africa, in their report 'Housing in Africa' estimated that appropriate housing throughout the continent should cost in the order of 2.5 times a household's annual income. See also Part 2, Paper 3

Of course this does not mean that such a large number of households are homeless and without shelter. But it does indicate that their contribution to the housing stock is not officially recognized, because their dwellings fall below a defined standard of construction, servicing or accommodation. Their houses may be unhygienic, illegal or considered temporary and unsafe. However the definition of officially acceptable standards often appears to account for the seeming hopelessness of any attempt to solve a city's housing problem. The official standards are impossible to achieve with the available public resources and to this extent seem arbitrary and unrealistic. A further examination of this apparent arbitrariness of standards and ways of achieving them would reveal that they were appropriate at another time or are pertinent to another place. They were borrowed or adopted, out of context, with little modification. Should housing be tested against set standards at all, and, if so, how should they be determined? What performances are to be met? It is not being suggested that cities of the Third World would have to lower their sights or that their citizens should reconcile themselves to environmental deprivation in perpetuity. What is being questioned are the instruments employed for the perception of urban problems and for their solution.

Housing standards

Urban administrations, including housing departments, are staffed by lawyers, economists, accountants, engineers, architects, physical planners, administrators and so on, each with their professional abilities and their own particular responsibilities. The role expected of, and played by, each profession, hardly varies from city to city. Furthermore, these roles are generally little different from those played by public sector professionals and administrators 30 years ago. If one was to examine the structure of urban government and administration of some cities, one would find little reason to suspect that the size or type of problems facing them had changed to any degree since 1945. The methods of revenue collection, powers of compulsory purchase, planning and building bye-laws and concepts of urban land use have hardly changed, despite radical changes in the character and population of the city. It will obviously be conceded, by an urban administration, that their problems have got bigger over the last two or three decades but there is little indication that they understand that the problems they face are not just bigger but in their change of scale have become fundamentally different. The provision of 1000 new dwellings per year may have been principally a task of construction but the housing needs of 20,000 new households a year present problems that cannot be solved just by building, even if the construction industry had the capacity. Amongst other things, it may involve reviews of the urban tax system, new approaches to land use, changes in legislation or public action to change the employment structure of the city. In a city that was growing at 0.5% per annum, the problems of water supply may have been a matter of good maintenance and occasional capital investment in civil engineering. But the provision of water in a city that is doubling its population every decade, is not just a question of routine public works.

Role of professionals

The staff of urban administrations have been trained in an educational system which, in general, has responded very little to the changing world around them. The curricula of many faculties of law and economics are much the same as they were in the 1930s; so are civil

Professional training

service examinations for administrators. Schools of architecture and physical planning have been closely modelled on, and often maintain affiliation with, those of Europe and North America, but do not appear to have come to grips with the unprecedented tasks that face them in their own cities. Thus a closed circle exists in which the schools and universities produce professionals for the administration and the administration dictates to the universities, through their employment structure, the type of professionals that they are to produce. Outside this circle there are new problems in need of redefinition and in need of new approaches to their solution. As long as their problems are erroneously assumed to be the same as those of previous generations, or the same as those of the cities of Europe or the USA and as long as solutions are sought in the well-entrenched remedies of the past, the citizens of the poor and rapidly growing urban agglomerations of the Third World will continue to suffer increasing deprivation.

NEW APPROACHES TO NEW PROBLEMS – THE DESIGN PROCESS

2

Housing is still widely considered to be principally an architectural problem. But, as pointed out in chapter 1, the settlement problems arising from rapid urban population growth require a wider approach involving many professional disciplines. The complexity of these problems necessitates the consideration of many different parameters such as land, finance, legislation, technology and political priorities which have to be assessed and weighed in the search for solutions. The solving of such multi-parameter problems should proceed in three stages:

the identification and analysis of the problem;
the synthesis of the components of solution;
the testing or evolution of results against their expected performance.

It has become customary to call this procedure a design process*. It is applicable to the solution of problems ranging from housing to health, from finance to farming, from pollution to politics, as well as to the problems customarily associated with the 'design' professions of architecture, engineering and industrial design. Buildings, machines and artefacts are *designed* using the same sequential process as that by which legislation is *drafted*, plans are *drawn up*, budgets are *prepared* and institutions *are set up*. A close examination of the activities of drafting, drawing up, preparing and setting up will reveal that they include, or should include, the systematic process of analysis, synthesis and evaluation. Therefore laws, budgets, plans and institutions are the result of a creative *design* act and lawyers, planners, economists, and administrators, in their roles as problem solvers, can be referred to as *designers*.

Design and problem solving

In common usage the term design has become mistakenly identified with the preliminary stages of the creation of physical products and the designer's involvement in the process of problem solving is thereby truncated in that the problem is identified outside of his part of the process by someone not further involved in the search for solutions. Similarly, the evaluation of the performance of the finished product is often excluded from the designer's part of the process. Thus the product of the designer's involvement has become the design not the solution.

Traditional limitations

* JONES, J. C., *Design Methods: Seeds to Human Futures*, Wiley-Interscience, London 1970.

9

For instance, an architect may be *commissioned* to design a hospital. He will be given instructions in a brief which will describe in some detail the facilities to be provided by the hospital and, to that extent, the solution is already anticipated. He will then prepare drawings and specifications for the construction of the building and supervise its erection, on completion of which his involvement ends. He will not be expected to evaluate the building either in terms of its performance in purveying curative medicine or as a solution to the problem of health for which it was commissioned. It is not being suggested that a single profession can or ought to take on the whole design process for a problem as complex as public health or housing. But it has been advocated strongly and frequently during the past 20 years that the whole *design team* should be involved in all the stages of problem identification, synthesis and evaluation of solutions.

Failure of problem analysis

The most frequent and the most fundamental failure in the process as applied to public sector issues has been in the identification and analysis of problems. As pointed out in the previous chapter, this has led to the irrelevant employment of tested solutions to what have been misunderstood to be traditional problems. To return to the hospital example, the architect, on receiving his brief, must assume that the health problem has been correctly identified and analysed as a shortage of accommodation for curative medicine and surgery and that the provision of a hospital as described in the brief could contribute to its solution. But a large hospital, however well-designed, will make little impact where the problem of ill health is the result of widespread malnutrition. Similarly, a programme of slum clearance will have an adverse effect, if in fact there is a shortage of housing due to population growth in the city. Again the encouragement of capital intensive industry will achieve little if a high rate of unemployment is a major feature of the urban economy.

Synthesis of components

The term 'synthesis' describes the stage of the design or problem solving process when components of the problem are matched with proposals for their solutions and brought together in a new order. For instance, the components of a public transport system including rolling stock, passenger flows, route networks, interchange nodes, schedules, staffing, management, financing and recurring costs are brought together in a feasible design proposal. Some theorists refer to this as the creative stage because it is here that potential solutions emerge through often unlikely combinations of components*. As pointed out, this stage is the one with which the physical design professions are traditionally identified. This may account for the past over-emphasis on physical products as remedies for complex urban problems. Designers are increasingly aware that the design process requires an understanding of whole systems, or of the chain of reactions which may emanate initially from a single action and advocate that many of the tasks of problem solving ought to be taken out of the hands of the single designer and entrusted to multi-disciplinary† design teams. This has led to a new approach to questions of communications that can span the languages and concepts of different professions.

* BROADBENT, G. H., Creativity, in *The Design Method*, Gregory, F. A. (Ed.), Butterworths, London 1966.
† Not to be confused with 'inter-disciplinary' meaning isolated contributions by various professions when called upon.

Over the last 15 years, a range of design methods have emerged which attempt to rationalize and generalize procedures. Physical planners were among the first theorists to emerge with a significant contribution to the externalizing of the design process. Patrick Geddes' famous description of the planning process as 'Survey, Analysis and Plan'* laid emphasis on 'diagnosis' or problem identification and analysis. However, it underplayed the process of 'treatment' or how to generate and evaluate strategies for the solution of planning problems. To redress this in the face of increasing understanding of the complexity of planning issues and of the demand for their public exposure, the profession set to work on the development of techniques of synthesis and evaluation as well as the sophistication of analytical methods. Since the early 1960s many different branches of analytical science have contributed to the understanding and language of the design process, including systems analysis, cybernetics, operations research, management techniques, mathematics and psychology. These sciences also confirmed that design was part of a wider process and could no longer be seen in terms of static goals.

In a complex and dynamic design situation, as required for the management of urban growth problems, it becomes a continuous activity. There is no final solution; not even a solution which will 'last for two or three years'. A change, albeit for the better, in one problem area will produce different and often unexpected problems in another. The solution to these may well in turn affect the situation of the previous one, and so on. The process is a continuous cycle of evaluation, analysis, synthesis and re-evaluation.

Design methods

Cyclic process

* GEDDES, P., *Cities in Evolution*, Edinburgh 1915.

3 APPLICATION TO HOUSING

The application of design methods (as described in chapter 2) to the complex issue of urban housing involves (a) an extensive analysis of the existing situation; (b) the establishment of a housing brief; and (c) the development of strategies to answer the brief. All this must form part of a continuous process of evaluation and feedback.

An essential feature of the analysis is the assessment of users' priorities of demand for housing and urban services. This is needed to prepare a series of briefs identifying the demands of different *Client Groups*. Only when these have been established should the city's public resources be examined to determine to what extent they can be used to satisfy the briefs. This order of investigations ensures that the search for viable housing strategies includes changes in the political, financial and managerial structure of the city administration, and not only the exploration of cheaper building materials and lower standards that is conventionally associated with attempts to solve housing problems.

The housing process flow chart

The flow chart (Fig. 1.3) illustrates this sequence of operations. The aim of the analysis stage is two-fold: it acquaints the design team with the nature and scale of a city's housing problem (housing need) and it reveals areas within the city that need a more detailed diagnosis, (areas of housing stress). An analysis of the locational, demographic and economic factors that describe the city's housing problem precedes the preparation of a phased programme for the relief of housing stress (housing targets). Simultaneous with this, the users' priorities of demands for housing can be established. The various demands expressed by households of different client groups are examined and are subsequently compiled in a number of *client briefs*. The design team's response to the various problems stated in these briefs form the basis of a number of outline proposals to be examined in terms of their feasibility before being assembled into potential strategies. The resulting alternative strategies are evaluated against public resources as well as public constraints in order to develop those most suitable in terms of benefits and costs to the community. The evaluation continues into the stage of implementation in order to provide the feedback for future analysis as well as to influence future proposals. The whole process is seen as a continuous cycle, in which the results of subsequent stages change the assumptions, predictions and intentions of previous operations. Each strategy is treated as an integral part of an ongoing process that has no end.

12

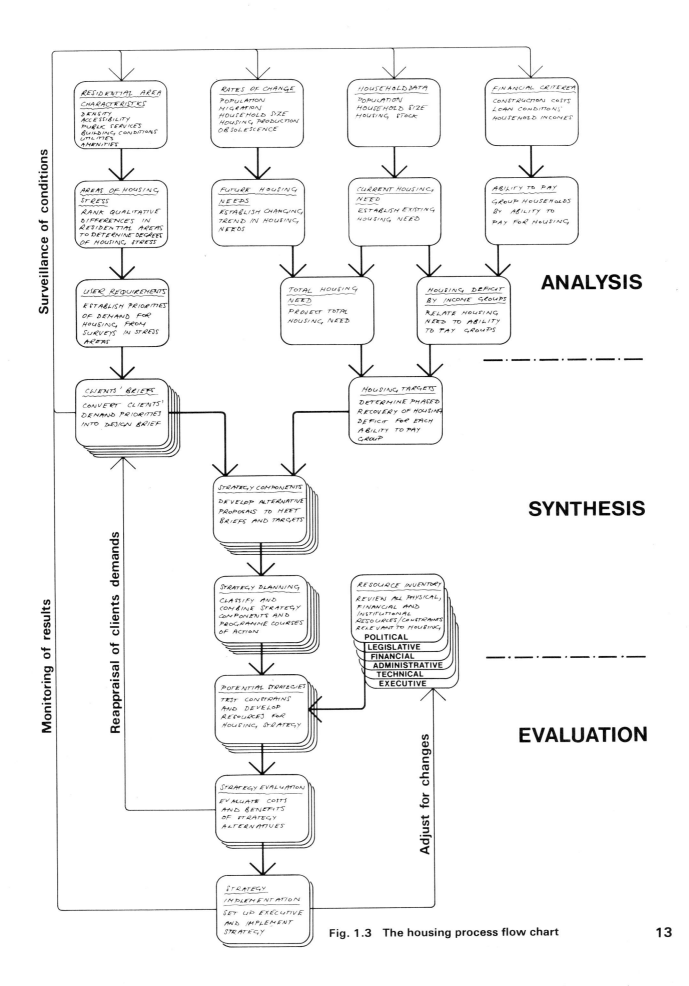

ANALYSIS

SYNTHESIS

EVALUATION

Fig. 1.3   The housing process flow chart

13

Reconnaisance survey

The start of a new approach to the design process of urban housing provision cannot be delayed while an exhaustive data bank is being compiled. Because of changing demands, it can never be complete, nor will the growth of housing needs stop while the 'existing situation is being sorted out'. The process is started on the basis of a quick *reconnaissance survey* on the firm understanding that this will lead to the establishment of a mechanism of continuous surveillance, feedback and review of the situation.* Urban administrations usually possess a great deal of information about the structure and infrastructure of the city. However, this is rarely in a form that will allow its immediate application to the definition of housing problems and it is rarely in one place. Essential information is often scattered amongst national, urban and private sector agencies responsible for the different public services. Official information tends to be often incomplete or out of date. This is no excuse to delay the process or problem identification. All that is needed at this stage is an overall view of the nature and magnitude of the problem and an understanding of changing trends.

Housing finance

A general picture of the ability of different income groups to compete in the housing market is essential to clarify the economics of housing. It can be obtained by relating the city-wide distribution of household incomes to the cost of construction and the conditions of capital financing. This exercise may reveal that a sizeable proportion of the city's households cannot afford even the most minimal or heavily subsidized dwellings that public housing programmes are producing. It will indicate the proportion of the population that cannot afford the present building standards and those who can afford better ones (see Part 2, Paper 3).

Housing needs

This description of the distribution of the urban population by ability to pay for housing does not indicate a city's housing deficit which is the difference between the total number of urban households and the number of dwellings deemed habitable. As pointed out in chapter 1, the standards which determine habitability are generally arbitrary and often have little to do with peoples' aspirations. Nevertheless at this stage of general analysis it provides a useful measure by which to assess the numerical size of the housing problem. However in view of the rate of population growth the present shortage of dwelling units is of little significance in comparison to future housing needs. Projections are needed not only of the future number of households, but also of the future growth or decline of the housing stock. The only indicators for these projections are trends from the past, which are generally somewhat unreliable guides. In spite of these difficulties it is necessary to make a series or range of forecasts as bases for the first tentative plans.

Housing targets

As a city's population grows the distribution of incomes, and therefore ability to pay for housing changes. Projections depend of course, upon speculations about the future wealth of the city and how that will change. Nevertheless it is important to attempt to take these changes into account in order to prepare indicative housing production targets that not only project the number of new units that will be required an-

* This principle was elaborated by O. H. Koenigsberger in his paper on Action Planning (op. cit.).

nually but also describe the markets for which they are intended. Obviously the further into the future projections are made, the more spurious they become. However, long term forecasts should be seen mainly as giving a direction. Their accuracy will not drastically affect immediate housing programmes (see Part 2, Paper 2).

City administrations know that a proportion of the urban housing stock is substandard and areas of slums and shanties are easily recognized by their appearance. But there are likely to be other sections of the housing stock where living conditions may be as bad or worse due to overcrowding, lack of servicing or inadequate public amenities. Such areas may go unnoticed by not being so obvious, but data on them are usually available, though they are rarely brought together and compared. Another task of problem analysis is therefore to collect and relate all the available indicators that can help to describe and compare different degrees of *housing stress* throughout the city. Such indicators should include the distribution of infrastructure, access to public transport, shopping facilities, schools, clinics and areas for recreation as well as the age and condition of dwellings, residential densities and occupancy rates. This list could obviously be extended though it is dependent on readily available data as there is neither time nor much advantage in conducting extensive surveys of the general urban housing problems during the reconnaisance stage (see Part 2, Paper 1).

Housing stress

This procedure for the identification of urban housing problems gives a general picture of:

>   the impact of the problem (who is affected);
>   the size of the problem (how many);
>   the nature and location of the problem (what and where).

It is not a sufficient basis for a brief for action to alleviate bad housing conditions or to provide housing for newcomers to the city. Only the users of housing or the *clients* can write a client's brief. The information used so far was entirely second-hand. Municipal standards deem a dwelling overcrowded if the occupancy rate of people per room exceeds an arbitrary norm. A building may be condemned as 'temporary' if its walls are made of mud; a household may be considered unable to pay for housing on the basis of one member's income, regardless of other members' earnings and contributions, and so on. The criteria used to judge the suitability of housing for its occupants are established by civil servants and professionals, not by those experiencing the extremes of housing stress, nor those in need of public sector assistance with their housing. The demands, values and aspirations of urban newcomers and other low income clients of public housing are often very different from the assumptions of those responsible for the design of housing programmes.

Housing demand

The next and most important stage of problem analysis is therefore to determine, through a series of interviews, the clients' demands for their housing. In cities of the Third World with a high rate of rural to urban migration a large proportion of the clients of public housing will not be urban citizens at the time of brief-writing. They will have to be represented in a series of *Client Groups* by those of their peers including friends and relations who already have an urban foothold.

Households surveys

15

The identification of areas of housing stress in a city indicates where the most deprived are likely to be found. It is reasonable to assume that, because of their inability to compete for the better serviced housing, the poorest of the potential clients will be found in those areas of the city with the highest degree of current housing stress. However, investigations should not be restricted exclusively to the urban poor. Household interviews to identify demand, will have to be held across a wide range of the urban population. It is essential that these interviews should form the starting point of a continuous monitoring of the changing demands and aspirations of different client groups.

The size of the sample and the distribution of household interviews obviously depend upon the staff resources available. Whatever these may be, economy of information-handling is important. For this reason, the designers of the survey must be clear about the principal issues that will constitute the housing briefs and develop techniques for obtaining and analysing the necessary information in the simplest and quickest manner possible. This is not an easy task as the briefs for each client group must not only state the group's demands but also rank them by order of priority. This entails obtaining responses to conditional questions from citizens who may have reasons to be cautious and wary of official interviews.

Client groups

The range of client groups is established on the basis of a series of demands expressed by people living under various conditions of housing stress. Their aspirations will be determined to a very large extent by their own experiences. For instance, a householder may state that if he had a choice he would like to become a public sector tenant. This may be for a variety of reasons. Perhaps as a private sector tenant he has suffered from a bad landlord and sees more security in having the Government as his landlord, not imagining that he could ever be an owner himself, or he may not want the responsibility of owning a dwelling.

Design briefs

The first stage of synthesis is to convert the lists of subjective demands of each client group into a set of objective instructions for design action: a brief. The briefs should, as far as possible, take the form of a series of *Performance Specifications* which stipulate *what* is to be achieved by any action, but do not restrict potential action by also stipulating in detail *how* it is to be achieved. A great deal of care must be exercised in the framing of performance specification clauses to ensure that on one hand they allow maximum flexibility to the house builder, but on the other hand they are precise enough to ensure that the required performance is assured (see Part 2, Paper 4).

The information, values and demands for housing analysed in the process of brief-writing are likely to alter many of the assumptions and statistics used in the initial reconnaisance survey. For example, the clients' concept of adequate shelter may differ from the official definition used to determine the urban housing stock. Its application may radically alter the housing production targets. Similarly, the range of urban households' abilities to pay may be found to differ from the income statistics used earlier.

Data feedback

It may not be possible to introduce immediate changes because of insufficient city-wide data but the process of continuous feedback and monitoring can start, as can the search for solutions to the housing problems perceived by the clients of housing.

In *client-oriented* housing programmes, the search for alternative strategies is centred upon satisfying the clients' briefs. Each will include target figures of the number of households to be accommodated over a given programme period as well as the clients' demands.

The next stage of the design process is to collect and classify all possible alternative courses of action that could contribute in any way to the solution of any one demand in any one brief. Because of the nature of urban housing problems the brief will include components ranging from security of tenure to the supply of water, from the availability of finance to the allocation of domestic space, etc. There are several ways of going about making provision for each brief component and the first round of elimination will be the test of each proposal against the clients' requirements. Those that cannot fully meet the performances specified by the appropriate brief clause are the first to be abandoned. Having a range of possible alternatives for the solution of each component the next stage is to put them together as a proposal for each client group which will as far as possible meet all their demands. In this process some ideas will have to be eliminated due to their incompatibility with other components of the proposal. For instance, a proposal for the location of schools may be found to be incompatible with the densities demanded by a brief concerned with the distribution of plot sizes. The advantage of considering each component brief separately before bringing them together in a united proposal, is that it encourages the search for new solutions. The discipline of breaking a problem into components before bringing together the solutions to each, reveals alternatives that otherwise would not be apparent. However, the result of the synthesis stage of the design process must be a unified proposal in answer to the housing demands of each client group. It is not enough to produce a series of sectorial proposals, one for the supply of water, another for the construction of dwellings, a third for the allocation of land, and so on.

Strategy components

The results of the synthesis stage of combining possible sub-solutions into proposals should be several alternative potential courses of action that would fulfil the clients' demands. Not until this stage, when a clear direction for the solution to a problem has been established, can a strategy be developed for implementation. It is important that no constraints outside the clients' brief are introduced before ideas have been conceptualized, otherwise the principal goals become obscured. Having reached this stage of synthesis, the proposals have to be evaluated against the resources available for their implementation. These are the political, legislative, financial, administrative, technical and operational resources of the city. They will be controlled on a variety of levels from central or national down to the resources of individual households (see Part 2, Paper 5).

Strategy planning

This list or inventory of resources contains the tools for action to satisfy the briefs. It enumerates all the potential resources that may be employed in the design of a strategy for housing provision as well as

17

potential constraints that may hinder the executing of strategies. The procedure which leads to firm proposals for action is, in essence, one of a series of cycles of testing of alternative proposals against the resources available in order to arrive at the most economic course of action. In determining what constitutes economy, designers have to make the value system they employ as transparent as possible.

Strategy evaluation

In the subsequent stage of bargaining it is likely that some of the clients' demands will have to be compromised in the face of competition from the conflicting interests of other urban client groups and the scarcity of material resources, particularly finance, skilled manpower and land. For this purpose, it is helpful to rank the components of each clients' brief, into 'vital needs' and 'less crucial demands'. To take an obvious example, access to water for every household must be rated as a vital need, whereas ease of access to a market may have a lower priority and can thus be compromised. Compromises should be seen as last resorts before abandoning a project. They should be considered only after the failure of alternative strategies to reconcile the demands for housing and the resources available to meet them. There may be situations where the demands of a particular group go against the welfare of the urban community at large. In such an instance it is the task of the professional to set up a forum in which the issues can be examined and the brief subsequently adjusted. This emphasizes the need for 'transparency' in the design process. The criteria for each decision, particularly those affecting the brief, must be established publicly. However, issues of 'public welfare' should not be confused with the exploitative interests of one group over another. An example is given in Part 2, Paper 6 which demonstrates the sort of conflict which inevitably arises between the demands of different client groups, the availability of resources, other interests in the city and the political aims of its administration.

Resources and constraints

The degree to which a client's demand can be met does not only depend upon the amount of material investment required for the strategy but often to a far greater extent upon the degree of institutional change needed and the political flexibility of the urban government. It will become apparent in the evaluation stage of the design process that many of the institutions originally conceived of as resources, actually constitute constraints upon the implementation of a strategy proposal. In some cases, these can be avoided or circumvented; in others, the proposed action will have to focus on the change of old institutions or the creation of new ones. However, institutional change is usually a lengthy process and, as stressed earlier, the pressure on housing calls for immediate action and cannot be postponed while new legislation is being enacted or new administrative machinery made operational. Housing strategies which are operational plans of action must be designed to include projects for immediate implementation as part of longer term programmes. These in turn are combined under an overall housing policy statement which embodies the fundamental principles upon which all action is to be based.

Monitoring

The evaluation stage includes a procedure for the monitoring of changing conditions, that is a continuous assessment of results in order to test the policy goals and to reappraise the briefs. The results of this evaluation are immediately fed back into the design process for the improvement of future action. A complete cycle is set up which, on one hand, must be flexible enough to introduce changes in the process, and on the other hand must be well enough defined to absorb changes without interrupting the production of housing.

This description of the design process as it would be applied to the formulation of urban public housing strategies makes no mention of the *designers* or the *design team*. That is deliberate. The professionals responsible for the design process and its implementation are of crucial importance to its effectiveness; but, the skills and the type of imagination required to house the urban poor are somewhat different from those traditionally taught and employed.

4 OLD AND NEW WAYS OF LEARNING

Design and learning

The design process as outlined in the previous chapters is also inherently a learning process. Educationalists refer to it, usually with different catch phrases, as the 'Enquiry Method of Learning'. Despite the common recital of such platitudes as: 'life is a learning experience' and 'learning does not end with graduation', little effort seems to have been made to formalize *real life* learning processes in education. Even schools of *design* are reluctant to employ the design (learning) process as the process of learning (design). An important contribution to design education was made in 1962 when a paper: 'Design Methods in Architectural Education' was given at a conference in London*. Although this paper was prefaced with the apology that its approach 'was originally intended as a teaching device and its first objective was therefore to produce designers rather than designs', the affinity between its theories and those of the design methodologists was revealing. More recently, there has been a growing co-operation between designers and educationalists which has brought about significant changes to the benefit of those institutions, that have seriously attempted to experiment with new approaches to teaching.

In 1964 Bloom published his *Taxonomy of Educational Objectives* which lists objectives against the behavioural criteria by which the attainment of each can be measured†. This received wide attention, particularly in those schools of design which had begun to involve psychologists and educationalists in their teaching. The recognition that the design process is itself a learning process and vice versa has produced a new emphasis on the importance of the process as opposed to the product. Thus, designers and design students are better equipped to learn and deal with problems, if they are able to observe and plan their own learning process. However, before expanding upon this, it is as well to outline the old, and still prevalent, approach to design education.

Role of project work

Project work has always been the basis of design and technical training. Its intended purpose has been to apply theory to simulated practice and to develop technical skills. Students are given a brief which states a problem, or more usually a symptom of a problem and they are given the

---

* THORNLEY, D. G., Design Methods in Architectural Education, in *Conference on Design Methods*, Jones, J. C. & Thornley, D. E. (Eds), Pergamon Press, London 1963.

† BLOOM, B. S., *Taxonomy of Educational Objectives*, Handbook II: Affective Domain, London, Longmans, 1964.

parameters within which they are to *design* a solution to it. In this way, not only is the problem predefined but the solution to it is often anticipated as well. Teachers of architecture may set a project with a brief for the design of a block of flats on a given site. They can be reasonably sure that the results of the exercise will be drawings for a building. They also assume that through the project they will be able to test the students' comprehension of the theory and techniques fed to them, prior to, or during the block-of-flats project. Indeed, it is not uncommon that such an exercise is set with explicit instructions to employ certain techniques, such as calculations for the main structural components or the detailing of the plumbing system. Similarly, students of engineering may be given performance specifications and a list of materials for the design of a machine. With this and whatever further information he is able to collect or recollect, the student prepares his solution to the brief in any way that he chooses and with occasional tutorial assistance. Finally on a fixed 'submission date', he will present for assessment the results of his labour regardless of whether he considers it complete or whether he had finished the project a week or two earlier. Finished or not, the drawings of the project submitted for assessment have to be beguilingly slick and final in appearance, for they are the product on which the student's design ability will be judged and marked. In the course of his training a student completes 10 to 15 major design projects. But that is not all. He will also attend several hundred hours of lectures in which he is presented with a body of theory and a catalogue of techniques compiled on the basis that they have been used and tested by the profession in the past. The information thus obtained is meant to be reinforced, in the student's understanding, by its application to the solution of design problems. This is rarely possible because of different emphasis given to the project briefs. But the method continues to be used to justify project work in the erroneous belief that solutions to design problems lie solely in the rearrangement of already proven technology, if not in the direct transfer of its previous application. This confusion may have its roots in the craft tradition, with its emphasis on technical competence, out of which the design professions have emerged. Until very recently, hardly any schools of architecture or design in Europe existed within the established university system. They were seen as belonging to the structure of technical training. However, now that they are 'in' they have to conform, particularly to the conventions of written examinations based on a curriculum of topics called knowledge. Together with the recent increase in technical information, this has led to a student's chances of becoming 'qualified as a designer', being dependent largely on his success in technical and theoretical examinations, usually with little pertinence to his ability as a problem-solver. Thus the role of projects in design education is still generally that of a support to the acquisition of technical and theoretical information. It is intended as a tool for the application of knowledge.

The design/learning process, on the other hand, reverses these roles. The project becomes a generator of needs for information, techniques and skills. The project is used to pose a problem, and the search for its solution generates a demand for resources. A great deal has been written about the very important aspects of *motivation, discovery* and *learning by doing* in the education of small children*, but little of it has filtered up to professional training. Without going into educational psy-

Project as generator of needs

21

chology and theories of student motivation, it is worth pointing to the amount and quality of information assimilated by a student when he is motivated by the need for it in order to progress with his *own* project. This is widely recognized to be far greater than in the more common practice where the student does not decide himself when he should acquire certain items of knowledge and often does not fully appreciate their relevance but has to take it on trust that they will come in useful one day.

The starting point in the learning process should not be a 'body of knowledge' or information but the statement of a problem to be solved. A student's first enquiry will be of where and how he can obtain the necessary information and understanding. Obviously, he will choose the most efficient way of informing himself, be it from a book, a fellow student, an outside consultant or his tutor. In other words, the student will have to organize his own way of solving a problem; he will have to design his own design strategy within the design process.

Role of the teacher   Contrary to common belief, the role of the teacher is of enormous importance in this context and requires considerable skill. His principal task will be to encourage the student to observe and to design his own process of learning. However there will be aspects of enquiry which need different emphasis in the student's self-motivated learning. For instance, a student may find it educationally unrewarding to understand the principles behind a particular technique and be satisfied with 'rules of thumb'. At the same time, he may see a need to get to grips with the theory of another concept that has caught his imagination. The part played by the tutor on such occasions is that of a 'sounding board' against which the student can test the rationale of his decisions and question them in terms of his objectives for his own education. At no stage in such an educational programme should the design procedure eclipse the learning process in order to reach a quick solution (or a product) which, in this context can be regarded merely as a tool in the learning process.

This may suggest that the teacher has a rather passive role. In reality, this is highly unlikely to be the case. In the initial stages, the teacher will probably have to pose a series of leading questions in order to 'get the ball rolling'. He may even have to suggest alternative approaches to provoke an entry point into the design/learning process. It is not reasonable to suppose that every student will automatically be stimulated by the statement of a problem. But it is reasonable to assert that somewhere in the design process every student will find an aspect that motivates him to pursue it to some depth of understanding, and this in turn will lead to other directions of search.

The selection of projects is of fundamental importance in terms of their

* BEARD, R. M., *An Outline of Piaget's Developmental Psychology for Students and Teachers*, Routledge & Kegan Paul, London 1969.
    BRUNER, J., *Towards a Theory of Instruction*, Harvard Belknap, 1966.
    ISAACS, N., *The Growth of Understanding in the Young Child*, Educational Supply Association, London 1961.
    VERNON, P. E., *Intelligence and Cultural Environment*, Methuen, London 1969.

educational and their social relevance. Just as 'problem identification' and 'brief writing' are part of the design process so they are essentially part of the learning process. Unless a student goes through these stages in his education, there is little chance of his being able to master more than the restatement of traditional solutions to familiar problems or the production of irrelevant proposals for the solution to new problems. It is frequently argued that there is a great deal to be learnt from examples of the past. This is true to the extent that the methods used in reaching solutions to problems can usefully illustrate the approaches of other designers. However, the overriding tendency is for students to plagiarize the products of famous designers with little idea of the real nature of the problems that were being tackled and with no notion of the problem solving process employed. This apprenticeship approach has lead to the emergence of predictable fashions of product styling.

Teaching traditional solutions

A visitor to a school of architecture, planning or industrial design may, if he did not expect it, marvel at the uniformity of the products and also of their presentation. It will probably occur to him that each student must have been given an identical task. This might lead him to wonder whether this duplication of effort was really necessary or to what extent each student can have benefited from the inevitable competition with his fellows. He will probably also notice that most of the designs displayed are familiar. He has seen or used similar products himself. On the walls of a school of architecture he will see the plans of hotels, public libraries, cinemas, airports and the occasional apartment block, or luxury villa. It may occur to him to reflect that the school being visited is in a country with an average annual per capita income of $200, 10% illiteracy and an urban growth rate of 6% per year. Our innocent but concerned visitor may continue to wonder whether these are really solutions to the country's problems of transportation, information exchange, entertainment and housing; and he may also ponder upon the very small proportion of the population who would be able to benefit from the results of the students' projects. He may also speculate upon what the graduates of such a school might do when confronted with a problem which is outside the established typology of past examples. Would they be able to respond to the housing needs of under-employed urban migrants? How would they approach a national school building programme? Could they identify the requirements for transport of peasant farmers?

Such questions raise the issue of using projects in the education of designers in order to generate an awareness of the problems most in need of radical design: the problems for which no tested solutions exist. At present many design schools, particularly schools of architecture, are in danger of producing *élite* professionals capable of being of service only to *élite* clients who constitute a minute proportion of their country's populations.

To redress this, projects in schools of design must be introduced in such a way that the students themselves define the problems for which they later write the brief for their continuing design/learning action. A student will therefore begin to divert his attention from physical objects to the performance of those objects, from the designing of products to the understanding of processes. The usefulness of what a thing does may

Products and processes

become a more important consideration than the thing itself. And because usefulness can only be determined by the user, the student will have to look beyond his own experience for the user's responses to his environment. He will want to know how people are using their tools, spaces and services and what are their demands for improvement. This implies that a large part of a student's education will take him out of the classroom.

Selection of projects

The way to approach the setting of projects is to examine problem areas of 'themes' as processes, such as 'Education' (not schools), 'Transport' (not roads or motor cars), 'Health' (not hospitals), 'Housing' (not houses). Within any such theme lies a wealth of projects and sub-projects from which a student can learn, or if necessary, a curriculum can be satisfied. Depending upon the students' level of understanding, project themes can be tackled at varying degrees of generality or specific detail. For instance first year students might handle a theme such as 'Urbanization' at the level of general understanding of urban growth rates and the resulting urban form, whereas more senior students could use the same theme to get to grips with the highly complex issues of rural to urban migration or the urban economy and employment structure. Alternatively different themes may be used to guide students from simple to more complex problems dependent upon the level of sophistication for which any student may be ready at any particular stage of his educational development.

A tendency has crept into the traditional design professions in which architects and planners see their roles as co-ordinators of all the various contributors to the design process, with no particular skills of their own, except those of synthesis and management. If we were to accept this view, any particular specialist training beyond a sound general education would be unnecessary. Even if this was so, it would be a mistake to assume that the learning process of project-based education was only applicable to the training of generalists. It would be equally wrong to believe that a specialist knowledge prevents one from being able to cope with wider issues. The building up of confidence to be able to look outside the narrow confines of a student's own specialization must be one of the principal educational objectives. Narrow specialist education has made it difficult for professionals to consider complex processes such as 'Urbanization' or 'Housing'. Their search for solutions remains within the confines of the traditional unrelated problem areas or sectors such as water supply (engineering), building (architecture), land tenure (law), credit facilities (economics and finance). It is not proposed that a new approach to education should try to create a super-specialist with a command of all the professional and technical skills needed to solve, single handed, the problems of urbanization or housing. It is suggested instead that students of any of these (and other) professions should be confident in outlining and evaluating strategies for the relief of complex problems. To do this they will have to be sufficiently familiar with the skills of a wide range of disciplines in order to know when to draw upon whom and to understand fully the role of their own specialization in the design process.

Though most of the illustrations given so far have been drawn from the physical design professions, they are in no way seen as the only potential beneficiaries of a project-based learning process. All professions with any role in problem solving, could and should benefit from basing their educational system on *generator of needs* projects. For instance a theme such as 'Urban Housing' provides a good basis for exploration and learning in sociology, economics, law and public administration courses as well as in schools of architecture, engineering and physical planning.

It would be interesting and rewarding if students from all these disciplines were to work and learn together on the project; all sharing the process of problem analysis and brief formulation and each contributing his particular interest or skill to the formulation of housing strategies. Unfortunately there are few, if any, multi-disciplinary educational institutions where group learning of this kind is possible. On the other hand, it is hardly practical and educationally of little value, for students, even of the same discipline, to attempt to undertake a project as complex as the kind of themes suggested, individually and in competition with one another. Group work is an essential part of the learning process.

Group-work

Each member of the group is responsible for a specialist role in each of the various stages of the design process. This allows individual students to study and solve a series of sub-problems and because of the synthetic nature of project work, the particular contribution of each, forms a significant part of the team's overall learning process. The success of this depends, almost entirely, upon the communication between the members of the team. Each student must have a chance to inform himself, not only of his fellows' findings and contribution to the project, but also of the methods used in reaching them. In this way students learn from each other in terms of gaining information and developing procedures and techniques. This exchange has to be formalized at frequent and regular intervals. These sessions should not only be used for the review of progress but also to discuss and plan the next stage in the project, its information needs and the work of each group member. Thus each student is involved in the whole process, but the unnecessary duplication of effort and useless competition usually associated with project work is avoided.

Division of labour

5

PROJECT-BASED LEARNING

The area of urban housing presents as diversified a theme for a learning project for students as for the professional staff of a city administration. The sequence of the design process is the same in a learning project as that described in chapter 3. The emphasis on the different stages of the process varies. It depends upon the aspirations of the students involved, not to mention the subject of other courses they are attending.

An initial discussion of the basis of the housing 'problem', without fail, revolves around households' ability to pay for housing and the size of the population who are apparently unable to join the market. The simple observation that slums and shanties are not desirable in a city invariably turns, or can be turned, to what is meant by *desirable* housing and what are the thresholds of amenities that deem a housing area a *slum*. The

Process of discovery

first task for students of any discipline embarking on a project of urban housing, is the examination of the city as a whole in order to identify *the problem*. The need to understand the size of the problem or the number of people involved, forces students to make themselves familiar with the main issues of population dynamics, growth rates and rural–urban migration. They have to examine the trends of household formation, the production of housing units in the city and the deterioration of urban building stock. This leads them into discussions of housing standards and the relevance of the concept of a housing deficit. The first understanding emerges of the importance of user requirements.

The second task is that of analysing the cost and financing aspects of the housing market. It provides an opportunity of appraising the economics of urban house production, and of examining the cost components of infrastructure, materials, construction, maintenance, management, fees, loan servicing, insurance and contractors' profits. In using the technique outlined in Part 2, Paper 3, students will come to grips with the relationships between rates of interest and amortization periods of capital loans and relate them to income distribution in the city. In doing this they discover that a large proportion of their fellow citizens have little chance of entering the officially recognized housing market. They also begin to understand the basic 'areas' of action needed to make housing available to more people. This promotes discussions of the limits of reducing capital cost by lowering space standards and construction costs. It also leads to considerations of user demands, the real costs of 'self-building' in sites and services projects and the limitations of building technology. Constraints of the market forces that control the

26

conditions of capital financing become evident, and this may lead the discussion to the subject of the distribution of wealth in the city.

The third major area of enquiry is into the physical fabric of the city and into the location of areas of *housing stress*. Facilities available in different parts of the city must be recorded and compared. To students with some knowledge of the city this may appear an easy task. They are familiar with the location of the principal slum and shanty areas. However, a discussion around the concept of *housing* as opposed to *houses* quickly reveals that there is a great deal more to peoples' living environment than just shelter and that the visual appearance of an area may be misleading. After enumerating the indicators that could be used to describe the characteristics of residential areas, students discover how to obtain the information they need and how to convert it into a usable form. The forum set up to decide the comparative ranking and **Exposure of values** weighting of the indicators invariably highlights differences in opinion and values amongst the students. This can be used to point to the even greater disparity in values which is likely to exist between the professional *producers* and the *users* of housing.

The different tasks of problem analysis can be undertaken independent- **Task groups** ly and a team of 20 to 30 students can be divided into three *task groups*, that would work simultaneously. The formation of such groups is not always easy. Many students want to be involved in more than one job, if not all three. Their dilemma will be overcome by frequent review sessions in which the whole team is kept informed of the discussions, decisions and the working of each group. Formal review sessions are es- **Review sessions** sential to ensure that the whole team is informed on, and concurs with, all that is going on. In this way the review sessions become teaching sessions where the students learn from each other. The introductions to demography, housing economics and spatial analysis are 'discovered' by the students while setting out to investigate apparently simple points which in turn lead to further and further questions of increasing complexity. Thus the traditional teaching device of introductory and theoretical lectures is replaced by enquiry methods generated by practical involvement in the project. This is not to suggest that the specialist teacher is no longer needed, but that his role has changed. Specialist advice will be sought by the students early in the project; in fact as soon as the process of enquiry reaches the point where common sense or the experience of the students can no longer provide satisfactory answers. Specialist teachers have to respond by becoming partners in the investigation. Teachers may 'steer' the search for answers in particular directions, but this is acceptable only as long as it serves the students' ambitions to handle their own projects.

Difficulties can arise in the timing of the first stage of the project when **Job co-ordination** groups are working simultaneously on different tasks. Although each area of analysis can be worked upon independently the conclusions of the different groups have to be co-ordinated. The results of the economic and demographic analyses must be brought together in order to establish the city's housing targets. The next phase of the project cannot be undertaken until the housing stress map has been finished. The housing targets, on the other hand, are not needed until briefs for each client group are prepared. With careful management the economic and

27

demographic analyses may overlap with the survey stage of a project. However it is much more satisfactory if, without curtailing the ambitions and the enthusiasm of some students or keeping others unemployed, all three tasks can be summarized together at a Final Review session. Because, at such a session, the main thrust of the housing problem is articulated by relating poverty and the resulting deprivation in housing facilities to the growth of the city.

Importance of user participation

The summary of the first stage of problem analysis or the introduction to the next phase should clarify the position: although a great deal of insight about the city's housing situation has been gained, a brief for action cannot be prepared without the participation of the clients. At this stage, many students tend to assume, not unlike many housing departments throughout the world, that their general understanding of the problem together with their own middle class aspirations for housing and urban services equips them to propose solutions. It should be stressed therefore that most of the major assumptions that had to be made in the first phase were those that directly concerned the users of housing. These included the proportion of income that could be devoted to rent, the sizes of households, and the priorities of access to services and amenities used as a description of housing stress. It is not difficult to see that such issues will determine the acceptability and therefore the success of any proposals, and that it is not enough to work on the basis of assumptions only. This is the moment when the project must move out of the classroom and into the homes of representative users of housing.

Location of surveys

The selection of survey areas is based on the results of the housing stress map and the various maps of residential areas characteristics, from which examples of problem areas can be selected for close examination. Students who have been involved in social surveys before, tend to be confident that they know what is entailed; but it is better not to rely on them completely and to emphasize at this point the special function of the survey in the design process. It is useful to start by examining the objective of the survey which is the identification of housing demands from different *client groups* and the preparation of a brief for action to meet it.

Sample size

A dilemma may arise concerning the size of the survey sample and its statistical relevance for city-wide conclusions. Educationally only quite a small sample is necessary to familiarize the students with the social survey techniques. The analysis of a large sample can become very tedious and threaten the morale of the team. On the other hand, to base the rest of the project on the responses of a very small sample obviously questions the credibility of the project and indirectly, therefore, its effectiveness as a learning experience. A delicate balance must be maintained between the reality or 'live' nature of the project and the efficiency and effectiveness of the learning process.

Information requirements

What information will be needed for the preparation of briefs? This question tends to stimulate lively and imaginative discussions resulting in long lists of information requirements. It is important to remind the team of the efficiency and speed required for this part of the housing design process. Examples can be drawn from the many detailed surveys that have traditionally preceded planning proposals and have yielded much data that was never used. This should lead to an examination of the basic differences between the activities of planning and of research; one being goal oriented, the other to test hypotheses. The interviewing of client groups is akin to a market survey, rather than to an open ended research survey, a difference which is often overlooked by planners throughout the world.

How can the information be obtained? This question is inevitably connected with the previous one. It introduces considerations of observation techniques, data gathering and recording. Much of the information needed concerns not only the social and economic characteristics of households, but also questions of demand priorities. Students will learn about techniques of interviewing and discover ways of preparing interview schedules and of analysing and correlating results in a meaningful way. They also learn to understand procedures of sampling and of conducting interviews. These skills can and should be outlined in discussion, but they can be really comprehended only in practice.

Just as it would be methodologically wrong to limit the problem identification to the analysis of second-hand statistical data so it would be educationally wrong to restrict this phase of the project to the classroom. The live nature of the project would lose all credibility if the clients' demand was simulated, and the students would lose an experience which is essential to their understanding of the real issues of urban housing. For many students, the survey is the first opportunity to have more than the most superficial contact with the more deprived sections of their own community. However well prepared a student might be for his first encounter with his clients, he invariably admits afterwards that the housing and living conditions of the lower income groups can only be 'experienced'. Apart from any deeper or broader understanding the students may gain from this experience, it contributes substantially to the development of the project. The students return from the survey with added confidence as advocates of the people with whom they now feel they 'share' an attitude. It is at this moment that, for many of them, the project becomes 'real' as opposed to an exercise. This conviction produces a sense of euphoria which is of great value to the students' morale and therefore to the progress of the project.

Live project

However carefully structured, the review sessions during and after the survey always break down into the recounting of anecdotes and the exchange of stories. These unrecorded observations often provide the key to understanding and interpreting the underlying reasons for various households' demands and thus play an important role in the preparation of briefs for action. Had the interviews been sub-contracted to employed interviewers these insights would have beeen lost to the designer. However, the students must be made to realize that such a survey cannot be conducted only by spontaneous conversations with householders. There is a need for a check list to ensure that the essential information needed for brief writing is covered in each conversation with householders. Students also learn from practice the difficulty of conveying and getting answers to conditional questions starting with 'if . . .' or 'supposing that . . .'. However, such questions are often the only

Personal involvement

way to introduce questions relating to peoples' aspirations or priorities of demand for the future.

It is important to get through the procedure for evaluating the survey data as smoothly and quickly as possible. The greater part of this work is routine statistical analysis which tends to become boring. There are several techniques for this depending upon the size of the samples to be analysed. One manual method which has proved successful with relatively small samples is to design the interview schedule as a simple grid in which each row represents a respondent and the columns represent the answers to questions. When complete all of the schedules can be pinned together as one large matrix. Apart from saving the chore of transferring information from the schedules to a matrix, this method has the advantage of reducing questions to simple catch phrases or headings. In conducting interviews the students are not tempted to read out a string of prepared questions, but have to formulate questions anew for each interview around a list of reminders.

Assessment of clients' demands

The identification of different client groups by their common demands is generally agreed upon in a stimulating session that tends to revolve around the informal contacts of the students with their 'clients'. This session can also be used to introduce the concepts and theories of group formation and social alliances. In this context, the statistical correlations of the survey data are important as a support. They help to quantify the different demands of each group. The task of preparing design briefs for each client group should be introduced by stressing the difference between peoples' demands for housing represented by the findings of the survey, and instructions for action to meet these demands which have to be incorporated in the brief. The students learn to look 'behind' the demands and aspirations of their clients by relating them to the present circumstances and experiences of each client group. This helps to make sure that the briefs are in answer to problems, not merely to symptoms of problems. For instance, a demand for a minimum of three rooms per dwelling may be a reflection of a practical need for a certain amount of space, or it may be an expression of a need for privacy between different parts of the dwelling, or a wish for a status symbol. Another type of problem arises when demand has been generated by the specific conditions of the interviewees and is not representative of the demands of the client groups as a whole. This is not an easy task and, as far as possible should be anticipated in the design of the interview schedules.

Brain-storming

With a design brief for each client group and a schedule derived from the housing targets, the search for solutions can start. By this time many participants inevitably have developed not only attitudes to the solution of their clients problems but also plans for specific solutions. This is the point at which to introduce a break in the continuity of the process and to open the definition of the housing problem and the search for solutions to an apparently irrational reappraisal. There are several ways of introducing this new element into the project, but the well-known technique of *Brain-storming* seems to be the most rewarding. Its aim is to produce as many ideas as possible that bear upon a defined issue. The principle upon which Brain-storming operates is association. One idea generated by a member of a group leads to or triggers off associated ideas in other members. By rapidly producing any idea that comes to mind the group can amass an impressive catalogue of alternative potential solutions to a stated problem. Any idea, by any member of the group, is welcome and therefore no criticism is allowed though of course ideas can be extended, refined or modified by other members of the group. Judging ideas should be avoided at this stage; evaluation will come later. There is no such thing as a silly, wild, speculative or stupid idea. It is easy to discard ideas. The greater the number produced during the brain-storming session, the more the chances exist of finding alternatives that can be developed. Each idea must be recorded as it comes up. This can be done by tape recording the whole brain-storming session, but this entails the tedius task of subsequent transcribing. An alternative is for every member of the group to jot down ideas on a card as he describes them. This system has the advantage of allowing frequent rearrangement of the cards when the ideas are classified. Classification is an extremely important part of the exercise though not always easy. A first attempt of arranging the idea cards into *families* should follow each session. The type of classification used depends upon the nature of the problems and the type of ideas generated; but the aim is to establish categories and sub-categories of the way in which ideas deal with each issue. When going through this task, it becomes apparent that the most valuable outputs are often not so much the ideas themselves as their classification. It has been found that a useful starting point is to list each idea by its field of operation in an Ideas Bank under the headings: political, legal, financial, administrative, technical, executive etc. (see Part 2, Paper 5). They can then be ranked into 'key ideas'(around which possible development into strategies may hinge) and 'support ideas'. These, in turn, should be linked within or across any of the categories and so on until possible courses of action begin to emerge.

Classification of ideas

There are many ways of starting a brain-storming session but it is important that everyone is relaxed. This is often difficult as even students who know each other well are often afraid of appearing foolish or unimaginative in front of their fellows. The brain-storming sessions should therefore be introduced as a break in the housing project, not to be taken 'too seriously' and treated as a game to be enjoyed by everybody. Any problem seems approrpiate for brain-storming provided that it can be stated simply and correctly. It depends heavily on the skill of the chairman to select the right sequence of brain-storming topics. This comes with practice, as does the group's adherence to the rule of disallowing criticism or judgement of ideas. A simple trick to get over the habit of responding to an idea with 'it cannot be done because . . .', is to encourage a response to start with: 'it could be done if . . .'. In this way concepts develop incrementally.

Group interaction

It is not surprising that the most creative and diverse brain-storming sessions are often those held with the least 'experienced' students. Previous contact with traditional approaches to the problem has proved to be a hindrance rather than an asset in the production of original responses to problems, even when posed in a new way. A technique that helps to get around the straight-jacket of a specialist outlook is to turn the topic of discussion away from the particular expertise. It is possible to use analogies for brain-storming instead of questions that directly incorporate the obvious issues of urban housing.

Brain-storming and the project

Brain-storming could be employed as a tool at any stage of the design process. It could help to generate ideas for the collection of information, the presentation of data and concepts or methods of analysis. However, the formal introduction of brain-storming at this point of the project makes an important educational impact by bridging the gap, so often left unspanned, between problem identification and proposals for action. Through the analysis stage, the students have narrowed down their view of the problem from an overall appraisal of the demographic, economic and physical characteristics of the city to the preparation of detailed briefs for particular client groups. The brain-storming quickly opens the project again to a wide range of considerations in preparation for the next phase, that of convergence into detailed strategy proposals. Where the survey has a morale boosting effect on the project by heightening its 'reality', the brain-storming usually has a similar effect by producing, without apparent effort, many useful ideas, most of which respond directly to the clients' demands. Unorthodox approaches to the problem become natural and even some of the most fantastic ideas can provide the starting point for feasible proposals.

The stage of designing housing strategies now enters the realms of the traditional designer and the project work of most planning and architecture courses. It must be approached with some care to avoid slipping back into the habit of emphasizing the 'product' rather than developing and understanding the process by which alternative strategies are developed and evaluated in order to reach a viable proposal. This is not to denigrate the importance of results as the culmination of the project. Indeed, the whole effort would be meaningless as a learning experience and in practice if it did not result in proposals for concrete action.

Strategic choices

Starting from ideas and concepts derived in brain-storming a series of alternative approaches are developed and tested against the clients' briefs. The physical, financial and institutional resources of the city are examined to establish to what extent they can be used to support the strategy proposals, and to what extent they will have to be re-organized or supplemented in order to do so. Finally a housing strategy flow chart can be drawn up showing the sequence of actions and indicating the field and level at which each decision has to be made. The principal educational objective is to demonstrate the complexity of decision making in the search for the best alternatives. Students must learn to stand back and observe their own decisions in the context of the goals of the project and their own learning process. The starting point, the Ideas Bank, contains a variety of 'key ideas' with obvious potential for meeting one or the other of the clients' briefs. There are ideas of a policy nature and others that have potential as components of a brief. None should be rejected at this stage. It is inevitable that certain directions appeal to some students more than others. It may happen that some ideas are abandoned, because no one is interested in pursuing them. This is often frustrating for the co-ordinators of the project who may try to persuade a group of students into a particular line of action. However, it would be educationally counter-productive to force a particular direction on the team.

Structuring of thought process

The Ideas Bank should be treated as a useful catalogue of areas of search. It is highly unlikely that it contains suggestions for every single aspect or stage of a housing strategy; but it should be combed for all entries that could possibly pertain to the goals indicated by the 'key idea'. These are then ordered by their level and field of operation and interlinked in their operational sequence. By completing a strategy planning chart (see Part 2, Paper 5), students will begin to understand the ramifications of what may have started as a relatively straight-forward idea. For instance, serviced land available on which householders can construct their own dwellings will be found to entail a great deal more than locating and purchasing land and preparing layout plans. It may well involve decisions to make adjustments in legislation, institutional changes in conditions of financing, reappraisals of municipal planning and building bye-laws, the design of social welfare and technical assistance programmes and many other major and minor measures of this kind. By programming in their proper sequence all the actions that lead up to the occupation of a 'sites and service project', the students begin to grasp the complexity of their proposals. By studying the institutional structure of the city as it impinges upon their project, they will begin to understand the forces that control and constrain radical changes in the provision of urban housing. They may well discover that the main thrust of design activity may have to concentrate on, say, the introduction of legislative changes and not on the provisions of infrastructure, as might have been supposed at the inception of the project.

At this stage the compilation of a Resource Inventory can be a useful device to test some of the proposals. This inventory entails the listing of all public and private institutions, laws, bye-laws and agencies that do or might impinge on any aspect of housing provision in the city. Once an institutional framework for a strategy is designed, several if not all the entries in the *resource inventory* need a close examination. This will provide a point from which to analyse the present machinery, thereby learning a great deal more about the management, control and administration of the city than can usually be imparted by lecture courses on 'Planning Law' or 'Local Government'. In addition, students will get an insight into the working of various voluntary associations, charitable organizations and popular pressure groups, so important to the provision of housing and community services.

Survey of urban resources

There are important educational reasons for the order of events which prescribes that proposals for answering the clients' briefs are worked out in some detail, before embarking on an assessment of the available mechanisms for the realization of the strategies. Students start by working out 'ideal' proposals to satisfy the briefs. In this way the demands of the users of housing will remain uppermost amongst the design objectives and will not get clouded by the blind acceptance of economic or institutional constraints. They will also become aware that solutions to housing 'problems' rest, to a very large extent, upon economic decisions and the need for change of inappropriate bureaucracies and legislation rather than upon the exploration of cheaper building materials and lower standards. Obviously, it is rarely possible for a group of students to develop every stage of their housing strategy to a point of completion. In the first place, the detailing of one set of actions will often depend upon the implementation of a preceding decision, though this may be assumed or simulated in the project.

Scope of project

33

Secondly, the students are not always able or interested in fully working out all the actions represented by the squares on the Strategy Planning Chart (see Part 2, Paper 5). This is unimportant, but what does matter is that they appreciate all the links in the chain between inception and implementation of a proposal. Students of architecture will concentrate their efforts on the physical implementation of a housing strategy, students of law on the legal and conveyancy aspects, students of economics on the design of economic and financial sub-strategies, and so on. But none should do so without a clear understanding of the context in which they are operating and the dependency and implications of their tasks in the development of the whole strategy.

Group co-operation

If the number of students allows, groups should be formed at the beginning of the strategies stage of the project to develop different courses of action. These may correspond to the briefs of different client groups or to alternative courses of action to meet the same requirements or to a combination of both. Apart from the added efficiency in the project of having several individuals working together to the same end, group work allows individual students to concentrate on different aspects of the strategy. Once a strategy planning chart has been devised by a group as a whole, each member will have a clear picture of the tasks ahead within which he can design his own particular contribution to the team effort. As with all the other stages of project, the success of group work depends upon close and continuous communication between the individual members of a group and between the different strategy groups. Otherwise tendencies will re-emerge for students to revert to their traditional competitive attitudes in producing results. The first review session after the outline strategy planning charts have been prepared is often of special significance and may result in a new group configuration. It is probable that some stages in each strategy will be duplicated by other strategy proposals and need only be worked upon by one group. There will be areas where different strategy groups or client groups will be in competition with each other, most often for financial assistance and land. After a *bargaining* discussion on these issues it may be found that the team should set up a separate group to go further into the major issues that span all the strategies and act as co-ordinating or policy agency. Different groups may be working on strategies that have different levels of operation. It is possible in such cases for one group to incorporate the work of another as a sub-strategy within its proposals. For instance, a strategy for the upgrading of squatter settlements may contain another group's design for a community action programme.

On no account should group work in the strategy development stage undermine the overall team approach to the whole project, nor should lack of communication between groups be allowed to affect the learning process. At the Final Review session that winds up the project, every participant must consider it a corporate effort which would have suffered without his contribution. The result must be presented as an integrated proposal for the satisfaction of the demands of the client groups. At the end of the project, many students tend to feel that they fully understand all the housing problems of the city and are confident that they know how to deal with them. As this is obviously not the case, the housing courses have been subject to the criticism that this method of learning deceived students into an arrogant confidence that will only be shattered when, in later life, they have to face reality. The counter argument is that no solutions will be found without confidence born out of an understanding of the unprecedented problems and demands of urban housing in fast growing cities. The foremost aim of education must be to develop confidence and understanding and not to overawe students into inaction.

6 ILLUSTRATIONS OF STRATEGIES

Housing in Urban Development was the title of courses run by the authors between 1973–75. In each case the project lasted for only six weeks and was conducted as an experiment in intensive group work, as well as a demonstration of project based learning. The length of the course obviously presented constraints to the depth to which any of the stages or topics could be pursued. It also meant that very careful preparation was required before the start of the projects. For instance, as much technical and reference information as possible had to be made available in order to minimize the time spent on routine data gathering. Standard sheets for the recording of the survey correlations, resource inventory and strategy planning were made available. And above all, a carefully programmed time-table had to be prepared. This, like an urban housing strategy, had to be flexible enough to allow for changes in the programme but well enough defined to ensure that a complete cycle of the process was achieved.

In some instances the participants had to take time off from the project for other activities of their normal curricula. This effectively reduced the duration of the project to as little as three weeks. The shortage of time in these cases did not appear to detract significantly from the learning process or the results of the project, though preparation and programming had to be even more thorough. However, the fact that the participants were doing and thinking about two things at the same time, and were having to cope with two approaches to learning simultaneously, considerably reduced the level of their involvement.

A number of interesting features emerged from the intensive courses. One of these is the possibility, presented by going very fast through one complete cycle of the process, of returning to any particular stage in order to pursue it in greater depth. For instance, one student of architecture was so fascinated by his one day experience of converting users' demands into a representative brief that he spent 6 months preparing a dissertation on the concept and use of performance specifications as opposed to standards. Others returned to the issues of comparative housing stress to examine further sophistications of the method experienced only very sketchily during the project. For most students the greatest gain lay in continuing work of the development of the urban housing strategies generated by the projects. The time available for the design of housing strategies never exceeded 10 days. In spite of this, some interesting alternatives were generated by students in answer to the problems and demands discovered by them in the course of the project. It would not be possible to go into the details of all the strategies for urban housing that emerged from these projects, but the principal ideas and directions of thought are recounted below to give an indication of the sorts of issues that were raised.

Seventeen per cent of the population of Bombay live in unauthorized 'hutment' settlements. A survey revealed a high rate of under-employment together with a high concentration of skills in building and related trades. This led the team to propose the formation of industrial co-operatives run by 'hutment' dwellers to produce building components for the growing official housing sector of the city. The resulting profits would be used for the improvement of their own environment.

Bombay

Industrial co-operatives

The predominance of down-town high density rented accommodation (60%) in Bombay has created a particular urban life-style. People living in 'Chawls' have easy access to urban amenities and are therefore reluctant to be resettled, despite their apparent overcrowding. Designs were prepared for high-rise blocks to be built on reclaimed land and over land belonging to the Railway Authority. Each block contained some accommodation to be sold for commercial use and larger flats to be offered to the wealthier clients, in order to subsidize the low income flats and make them financially viable.

High density mixed development

One of the older communities of Bombay, the fishermen, are under constant pressure to give up their commercially valuable land in the down-town areas. This put them into a dilemma, as it threatens their occupation; but, at the same time, it offers them extra money for improving their fleet and equipment. As a compromise, the team worked out a suggestion to float these communities on pontoons in the shallow bay waters. This included a proposal for intensive fish farming to supplement their deep sea fishing.

Land substitution

More than 50% of the employed population of Chandigarh work for the Government which entitles them to housing for which they pay 10% of their income in rent. However, due to shortages, Government-owned dwellings are only available to half of those entitled to them. The remainder house themselves in the private sector for which they receive an additional 12% of their salaries as a housing allowance. This costs the Government £600,000 per annum. The strategy proposed that the Government should provide incentives, in the form of a 10 year exemption from property tax, land and building materials at controlled prices and a capital loan at 6% interest over 16 years, to small entrepreneurs to build two-unit dwellings. This assistance is conditional on one of the units being let to the Government for a period of 10 years at a fixed rate calculated on the basis of the present average rent of Government quarters. The other unit can be occupied by the owner or let at the market rate. The rent subsidy saved by the occupation of the Government rented units' by civil servants presently finding their own accommodation would be used to service the seed capital loan needed to start the programme and later to prime a revolving housing fund. If the 'Chandigarh Housing Scheme' (C.H.S.) had been started in 1974 with 850 units on a Central Government loan at 6% interest, it would become self-supporting by 1990 with an annual production of 5000 units. Figure 1.4

Chandigarh

Revolving fund

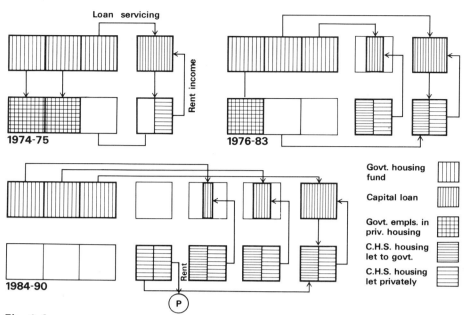

Loan servicing

Rent income

1974-75

1976-83

Rent

1984-90

P

Govt. housing
fund

Capital loan

Govt. empls. in
priv. housing

C.H.S. housing
let to govt.

C.H.S. housing
let privately

Fig. 1.4

schematizes the flow of cash and Government tenants over the initial
phases of the scheme.

Rationalized land use

Large areas of land in Chandigarh designated for recreational use are
neglected by the local population and are therefore lying vacant and un-
maintained. A strategy suggested the re-allocation of those 'green'
areas on the basis of the actual number of potential users of the
recreational space in each neighbourhood. This lead to the freeing of a
considerable amount of land for urban agriculture as well as for the
settlement of the 'informal' service sector population, presently not
catered for and therefore having to live in unserviced slums on the city
fringes.

New town settlement

As a new town, all Chandigarh's population are 'newcomers', but very
few of them are in a financial position to move straight into officially
recognized housing. It was therefore proposed to lay out special 'transit
camps' for the reception of migrants with a programme for their gradual
upgrading by the occupants. In this way the settlement process of the
poorer communities is made part of the city's overall development.

Baghdad

Rationalized
infrastructure

The most common complaint made by households interviewed in
various parts of Baghdad related to the state of municipal services of
sewerage, stormwater and public open space. After investigating these
complaints, the student teams proposed a number of long-term policies
combined with immediate actions for the collection and recycling of
garbage and of sewage effluent on a self-supporting basis, and the construction of a series of canals for irrigation of parks and open space as
well as for stormwater drainage.

New low-income
housing

The household survey in Baghdad established that low-income
households are willing to spend up to 25% of their income on housing.
This is still not enough to provide the larger households with adequate
accommodation. The team therefore felt that, like health and education,

38

housing should be available by need rather than by income and as such would have to become the concern of the national government. Calculations revealed that in charging a flat rent of £10 per month over 20 years, the losses incurred by the larger dwellings would be more than offset by the profits accruing from the smaller ones.

A locational study suggested that the new housing should be developed in phases, at first using up all land that was already allocated and laid out as plots though not developed, and then filling in those areas between housing that would require a minimum of new infrastructure. The result of this plan showed that the City of Baghdad could house twice the expected population growth for the next 25 years within its present confines using only single storey construction, and saving a large capital investment in infrastructure.

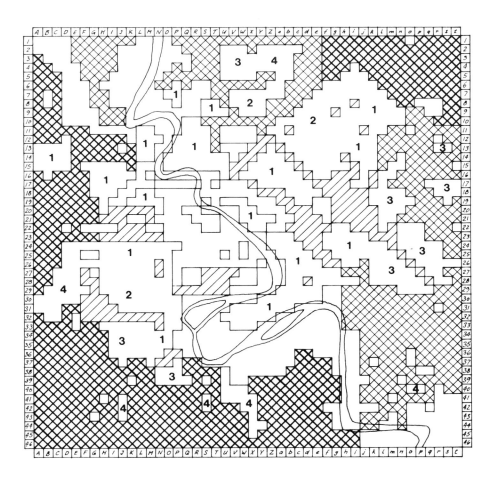

Fig. 1.5   Baghdad 1974 (0.5 km grid). **Land for residential development** (potential surface map).

    ☐ Infill development 1: 75–100% built up
                                2: 50–75% built up
                                3: 25–50% built up
                                4:   0–25% built up
    ▨ Phase I development
    ▨ Phase II development
    ▨ Phase III development
    ☐ Other uses, such as industrial, commercial, recreational etc.

Building clinic

The household surveys in Baghdad revealed a dominant demand from householders for assistance with the planning, construction, extension and maintenance of their houses. There was a particularly obvious need for this in Thawra City, a high density site and service scheme started in 1961 and now accommodating more than 800,000 people. While working on a proposal for the establishment and staffing of a technical advice unit, the team realized that such a venture could be started on a voluntary basis by students of architecture and so it became a realizable strategy. The proposal for a 'Building Clinic' staffed by a rotation of senior students was welcomed by a Social Research Centre established in Thawra, who offered local accommodation, support and publicity. This clinic was to operate for two days a week in the first instance. The team worked out a system of record keeping and registration of 'cases' for the 'clinic'. They made a survey of the sort of problems that were likely to need treatment most frequently and started to outline the types of solutions most appropriate to them. The scheme was introduced to all their fellows in order to recruit volunteers and to the teaching staff in order to show the educational potential of a continuous live project of direct service to the community.

Bangkok

Community action game

140,000 households in Bangkok have no title to their place of residence and are thus under a constant threat of eviction. A survey conducted in one of the largest squatter areas revealed that security of tenure was the first priority amongst their demands. The team approached the problem by developing a strategy that could present and clarify the possible areas of action to be taken at community level to tackle problems of the threat of eviction; secondly to force Government agencies to respond to the problems; and thirdly to motivate squatters to establish their own agencies.

The problem involved a large number of organizations and individuals. Innumerable decisions were needed for every possible course of action. The bargaining process was represented in a flow chart. The team decided to use the technique of *gaming simulation* as the best way to study the various possible actions involved in the organization of a community action programme (Fig. 1.6.). The game used as starting points actual events of the recent past in Bangkok. A critical situation—the threat of eviction—was chosen as a trigger mechanism. This stimulated a first round of decisions that could lead to a number of intermediate results. Some of these did not change the original situation and made it necessary to start again. Others provided a trigger for further rounds of decisions, the outcome of which eventually lead to three types of housing programmes. It was seen as an educational tool for students as well as for squatter communities.

Community building societies

In the event that some form of security was granted, the Bangkok squatters expressed a strong desire for improving their domestic as well as their communal living conditions, but felt unable to do so without assistance. Sceptical of proposing yet another city level bureaucracy working from the top down, the team worked out a proposal for the establishment of Community Building Societies operated by 100 to 200 households. These relied upon the concept of a 'social collateral' to avoid the need for heavy capital security.

40

Bangkok's liberal land policy had made it impossible for public sector agencies to cope with the rising costs of land for residential development. A long-range policy that implied Government intervention in the land market was therefore suggested. The municipality would acquire, while it was still available at low prices, peripheral land for the next 15 years, develop it and redistribute it on leasehold at rates high enough to be profitable but much lower than current urban market prices.

Land bank

As a rapidly growing industrial venture, Ahmedabad is continuously in need of new labour. Lack of co-ordination between the supply and demand of labour has resulted in underemployment and the growth of uncontrolled settlements. It was therefore suggested to set up a series of *reception centres*. These were to be equipped with training facilities for various trades and combined with an efficient labour exchange office which would monitor the demand of skills from industry.

Ahmedabad

Reception centres

A survey amongst the industrial labourers who constitute more than half the workforce of Ahmedabad proved that, having crossed the hurdle of securing a job, workers were unable to satisfy their housing needs unaided. Students felt that factories, largely responsible for the growth of this proletariat, should be made responsible for housing their own workers. It was calculated that an average-sized factory could provide housing for their employees within a period of 10 years, by using its own reserve land and recovering the capital outlay by a 5% deduction from the wage of each worker housed.

Industrial workers housing

During the rapid growth of Ahmedabad a number of villages were 'overrun' by the industrial as well as residential development around them. With the exception of access to a few services, these enclosed communities remained isolated from city life. Rather than suggesting to remove them against their will, a strategy was developed for the gradual social and physical integration of these communities through a number of technical, legal and financial assistance programmes under their own management.

Urban villagers

Large areas of Nairobi that were laid out by the colonial administration before independence have extremely low residential densities and a very high level of servicing. The team proposed that the city rating structure be changed in order to tax underdeveloped plots and gardens larger than half an acre. This would encourage the private sector to put serviced land on the market and to construct housing, principally for the middle income groups who suffer from an acute housing shortage.

Nairobi

Rate restructuring

The Kenya Regulation of Wages and Conditions of Employment Act stipulates that all employers must contribute to their employees' housing. But control of this legislation is difficult to maintain. The team proposed that this be reconstituted as a housing tax which would then be redistributed centrally to all registered employees on the basis of a fixed norm, as a Housing Allowance. The surplus from this would provide seed capital for a revolving fund which, without external financing, could produce 16,000 new dwellings a year in 10 years' time.

Employees housing tax

50% of the respondents to the household survey conducted in Nairobi were to some extent dependent on family connections in rural areas or

Urban agriculture

41

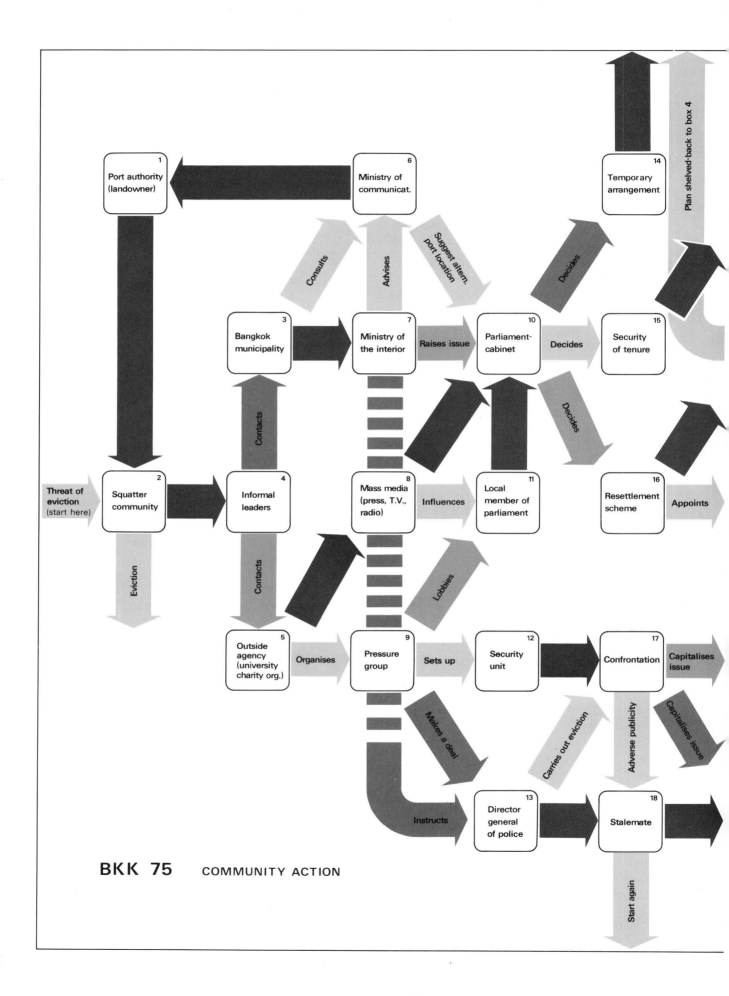

| 1 Port authority (landowner) | | 6 Ministry of communicat. | | 14 Temporary arrangement | Plan shelved-back to box 4 |

Consults
Advises
Suggest altern. port location
Decides

| 3 Bangkok municipality | 7 Ministry of the interior | Raises issue | 10 Parliament-cabinet | Decides | 15 Security of tenure |

Contacts

Decides

Threat of eviction (start here)

| 2 Squatter community | | 4 Informal leaders | | 8 Mass media (press, T.V., radio) | Influences | 11 Local member of parliament | | 16 Resettlement scheme | Appoints |

Eviction

Contacts

Lobbies

| 5 Outside agency (university charity org.) | Organises | 9 Pressure group | Sets up | 12 Security unit | | 17 Confrontation | Capitalises issue |

Makes a deal
Carries out eviction
Adverse publicity
Capitalises issue

Instructs

| 13 Director general of police | | 18 Stalemate |

Start again

BKK 75   COMMUNITY ACTION

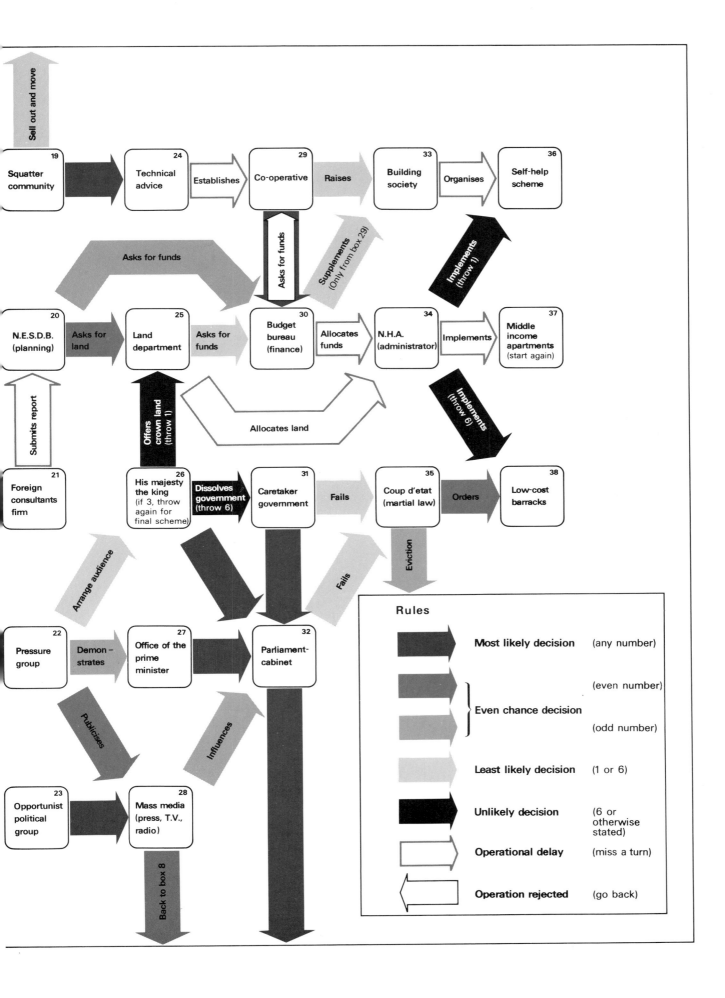

expressed a need to be able to supplement their urban earnings by growing foodstuffs. To satisfy this need, the team recommended new types of housing estates on the edges of the city with individual market gardens attached to the houses. If it becomes necessary in future, such estates can be developed for high density housing with minimal additional investment in infrastructure.

TOOLS AND TECHNIQUES

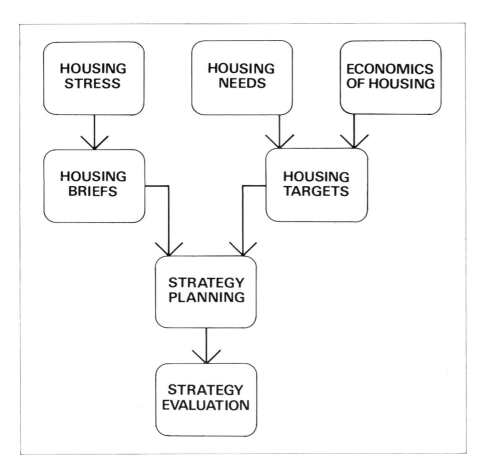

This set of papers brings together a number of tools and techniques relevant to the Housing Process. Each paper describes how to go about implementing one of the stages of a client-oriented housing process, but the techniques described in them lend themselves to more general usage as well, and with appropriate modifications, can also be applied to fields other than Housing. Each paper is self-contained, but the reader is asked to refer to the main body of the book for the background to the concepts used (e.g. client orientation). Each paper examines the problems and issues of one particular stage and presents an appropriate technique for its execution. Reference is also made to tools and techniques that were developed by others for purposes other than a client-oriented housing process, where these are thought to be capable of being used with modifications.

The papers of Part 2 are seen as serving two purposes. For the professional they are meant to act as the 'back of an envelope', enabling him to work out, reasonably accurately, the parameters of the problems involved, on the spot, without recourse to massive data-hunts or sophisticated hardware. Secondly, for the student/teacher, they are techniques that allow an impression of the total picture to be obtained in a way that is designed to allow the rapid testing of numerous assumptions. It is hoped that by thus demystifying the consequences of different decisions, a greater understanding of the techniques will emerge and lead to the development of further sophistications and variations by the user himself.

The papers* are arranged in the sequence in which it is suggested they be used. A simplified diagram of the design process for housing is shown at the start of each paper. The first stage of *Analysis* involves looking at the city in order to asses: Where the problem is, What it is, How many are affected by it, and What resources are required and are available to overcome it. Stage 2 is that of *Survey*: How to identify in detail the problems, in and of, various localities, how their occupants see them, and then how to convert them into a working brief. Stage 3 examines how to go about finding solutions to those problems by developing *Strategies*. Stage 4 is one of *Evaluation* of alternatives proposed in order to recommend relevant strategies for *Implementation*.

* Paper 3, *The Economics of Housing* was contributed by D. A. Turin, London Master Builders' Professor of Building at University College London.

RESIDENTIAL AREA CHARACTERISTICS

A method for the comparative analysis of the conditions and infrastructure of urban residential areas to establish degrees of 'housing stress'.

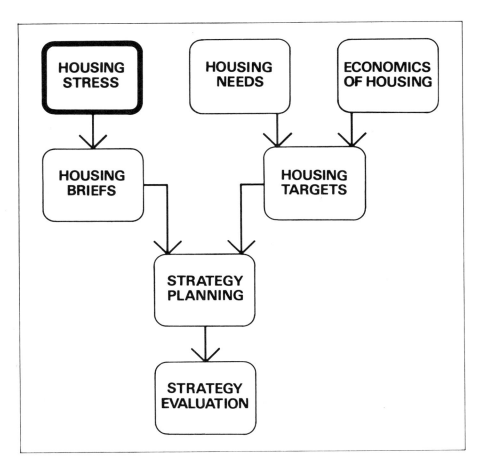

The first step in the preparation of a strategy for urban housing is to become familiar with the characteristics of the housing provision that already exists in the city. This should be done for the city as a whole on a comparative basis. Most citizens will be familiar with some of the apparently worst housing areas such as eye-catching squatter settlements and they will probably know where the richest or most influential people live. But few urban authorities have information on exactly how bad all the housing facilities are in the 'worst' areas or even the location of all of them. Often people live under intolerable conditions but their plight is not realized because the fabric of their dwellings is not dramatically indicative of their lack of space or facilities. Apparently satisfactory housing areas may be in danger of becoming run down because of the inadequacy of services or amenities.

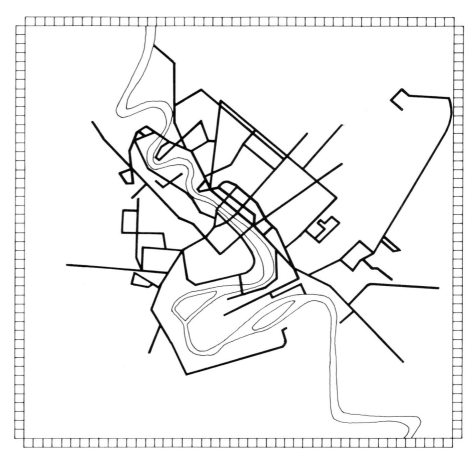

Fig. 2.1 Public transport routes (0.5 km grid)

The technique described below is a simple reconnaissance survey tool for the preparation of a series of housing area characteristic maps and for their combination into a housing stress map. The results are a crude but very useful sketch of the characteristics of urban residential areas which give the designer an invaluable starting point from which to go into greater depth in analysing housing problems and formulating housing strategies for different client groups of a city. The Housing Stress Map technique is *not* a substitute for a survey of actual user demands in a 'client-oriented' approach to urban housing. But it is an aid to identifying the major categories of client groups for housing and their probable locations throughout the city.

There are many indicators that can be used to describe the different character or degree of provision of housing facilities such as:

> age and condition of buildings;
> availability of water, sewage and drainage;
> accessibility to daily shopping, schools, medical facilities and public transport;
> accessibility to public open space and religious and recreational facilities;
> residential densities and occupancy rates etc.

Such indicators can be used directly to describe the physical quality of the environment and the provision of services and amenities. Others

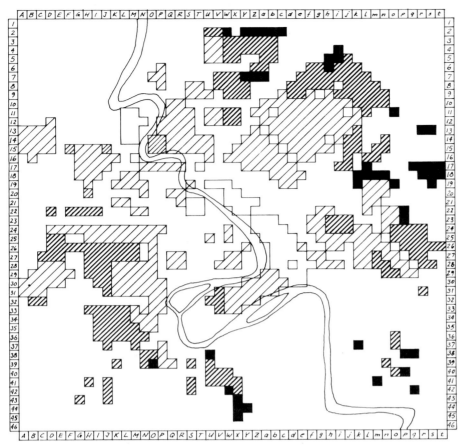

Fig. 2.2 Access to public transport (0.5 km grid)
- ☐ less than 10 min walk to more than 3 buses;
- ◨ less than 10 min walk to 2–3 buses;
- ▨ more than 10 min walk to 2–3 buses;
- ▩ less than 10 min walk to 1 bus;
- ■ more than 10 min walk to 1 bus.

such as suicide rates and incidence of delinquency are also felt, by many urban sociologists to be indicators of social deprivation caused by unsatisfactory living conditions but as indicators they are more difficult to interpret.

At this stage of the housing process time and effort should not be wasted by attempting to carry out extensive surveys in the field or to update information that is two or three years old. This will come later. The intention of the reconnaissance survey is to get a quick overall view of the housing situation of the city. Almost every city authority has some recent data on land use and the extent of its physical infrastructure. But such information is unlikely to be available in such a form that immediate comparisons can be made between each indicator. Therefore the first step after collecting the basic data maps, charts, tables, diagrams and reports is to convert them into a common language. There are various ways of doing this but the one described below has been tested in several cities and has proved to be simple to use and reliable as a reconnaissance survey technique.

Each square of the grid represents an autonomous area whose characteristics are to be described. Therefore the smaller the grid the

Residential area characteristic maps

Construct a grid over a land-use map of the city	greater the accuracy. However, the characteristic maps will only be as accurate as the data which is applied to them. And the more grid squares used the more complicated becomes the process of preparing and evaluating the maps. Figure 1.2 shows a 0.5 × 0.5 km grid over a map of a city. The area covered is *c.* 500 km^2.
Pick out and code those grid squares predominantly covering residential areas	Although one is principally interested in residential areas, it is very useful if the dominant land-use of other areas is indicated (such as commercial, industrial, recreational, waste land, farm land, etc.). For identification each square of the grid should be coded along the *x* and *y* axes of the map.
Agree a range of scores and apply them to each indicator	Each indicator must be divided into a number of units and given a score whereby the least favourable conditions get the highest score and the best conditions get the lowest score. For instance, Fig. 2.1 shows a map of public transport routes. This information has been converted into degrees of accessibility to public transport in order to relate it directly to residential areas. The key to the map (Fig. 2.2) shows that a score range of 1–5 was used, the highest score indicating those areas with the least access to transport.

It is important for ease of computation of housing stress (see below) that each indicator should fall within the same range of scores though each need not necessarily have the same number of subdivisions. For instance it may be felt that accessibility to public open space should only be boken down into three categories whereby:

more than 10   min. walk to p.o.s.—Score 5
         5–10   —   3
less than   5   —   1

Plot characteristic scores on grid map	A suitable hatching or colouring should be chosen for each score so that the differences between the score gradations can be read easily when applied on the maps. A separate map should then be completed for each indicator by hatching each grid square that covers a residential area with the score that applies to that square.
Complete residential area characteristic score chart	A table should be prepared which records the numerical score of each grid square for each indicator and the scores should be recorded on this (see Fig. 2.3). Though the score chart and series of maps that emerge from this stage of the process record the same information they are both useful for different reasons. The series of maps give an immediate visual impression of the city structure and the different characteristics of each residential area. The score chart is needed for the computation of the housing stress values (see below).
Housing stress map Agree weighting factors for each indicator	The housing stress map is a combination of all the indicators of residential area characteristics. Basically the scores for each indicator of each grid square are added up and plotted on the housing stress map. But before this can be done allowance must be made for the relative importance of each indicator. For instance one residential area may have a score of 4 for availability of water and a score of 2 for condition of roads. If these two scores were simply added the good condition of roads would in terms of housing stress eclipse the fact that there is an acute

Grid ref.	Residential density	Condition of buildings	Access to primary school	Access to clinic	Access to local shop	Access to amenities	Access to public open space	Water supply distribution	Drainage distribution	Access to public transport	Stress score
Weighting factor											
A1	3	3	2	1	2	2	2	1	1	3	
A2	3	4	2	2	2	1	2	1	1	3	
A3	2	3	1	3	3	2	3	1	1	2	
A4	1	2	2	2	4	2	3	3	2	3	
A5	1	1	2	3	3	1	2	2	2	2	
A6	1	2	1	2	3	1	1	1	1	3	
A7	5	5	4	3	2	5	4	4	5	4	
A8	5	4	3	3	4	5	4	4	5	3	
A9	3	2	3	2	5	4	3	4	4	4	

Fig. 2.3

Grid ref.	Residential density	Condition of buildings	Access to primary school	Access to clinic	Access to local shop	Access to amenities	Access to public open space	Water supply distribution	Drainage distribution	Access to public transport	Stress score
Weighting factor	14	9	7	3	6	2	3	10	8	8	
A1	3 42	3 27	2 14	1 3	2 12	2 4	2 6	1 10	1 8	3 24	150
A2	3 42	4 36	2 14	2 6	2 12	1 2	2 6	1 10	1 8	3 24	160
A3	2 28	3 27	1 7	3 9	3 18	2 4	3 9	1 10	1 8	2 16	136
A4	1 14	2 18	2 14	2 6	4 24	2 4	3 9	3 30	2 16	3 24	159
A5	1 14	1 9	2 14	3 9	3 18	1 2	2 6	2 20	2 16	2 16	124
A6	1 14	2 18	1 7	2 6	3 18	1 2	1 3	1 10	1 8	3 24	110
A7	5 70	5 45	4 28	3 9	2 12	5 10	4 12	4 40	5 40	4 32	298
A8	5 70	4 36	3 21	3 9	4 24	5 10	4 12	4 40	5 40	3 24	286
A9	3 70	2 18	3 21	2 6	5 30	4 8	3 9	4 40	4 32	4 32	266

Fig. 2.4

shortage of water in the area. To overcome this a series of weighting factors for each indicator have to be decided upon. Care must be taken to minimize subjectivity in the allocation of weighting factors. One person may feel that the provision of water is the most important factor in housing while another may think that occupancy rates showing degrees of overcrowding are more indicative of stress in housing areas. In order to reduce the subjectivity of individual bias, as many people as possible should take part in reaching a concensus on the weighting factors for each indicator. Therefore every member of the planning team should be involved in this stage of the process. In allocating weighting factors the degree of accuracy of information on which each indicator has been based should be considered in addition to its relative importance. In the example shown in Fig. 2.4 the indicator 'Access to Amenities' which included leisure and religious facilities was given a weighting factor of 2 out of a possible 15. Though the team felt this was an important indicator, the information from which the Residential Area Characteristic map was drawn, was not as reliable as for other indicators so the weighting factor was reduced from 6 or 7 to 2 in order to minimize distortions to the Housing Stress map.

Calculate and present housing stress scores

Having agreed the weighting factors for each indicator, the individual scores should be multiplied by them for each score and added to the score chart. Then the weighted indicator scores can be summed for each grid square to produce the final housing stress scores (see Fig. 2.4). These can then be applied to a copy of the grid map of the city to produce a Housing Stress Map. Though each indicator will only have had a score range of, say, 5, the range of stress scores may be in the order of 500, which is an impossible range to depict graphically though it is recorded to the nearest digit on the score chart. Therefore the stress score range presented on the map will have to be simplified (see Fig. 2.5).

The resulting Housing Stress Map shows at a glance those areas of the city under greatest degrees of housing stress and those that are better serviced. However, the Housing Stress Map cannot be used on its own. Constant reference must be made to the maps of residential area characteristics in order to check which of the indicators predominate in accounting for the stress score of any particular area. For example, an area may have a high stress score because of a lack of public amenities though the condition of buildings and domestic services is satisfactory, while another area with a similar stress score is a squatter settlement of temporary shelters but having good access to services and amenities. Stress in a third area may be the result of severe overcrowding indicated by high densities combined with high occupancy rates despite good physical conditions and so on.

The technique is based on criteria of housing need determined by the value systems of middle-class professionals. However well-intentioned and well-informed, these values are unlikely to represent the demands of all economic and social groups in the city. These must be checked and fed into the process as the next stage of a client-orientated housing process.

Potential surface technique

The technique as described above is used to identify the characteristics

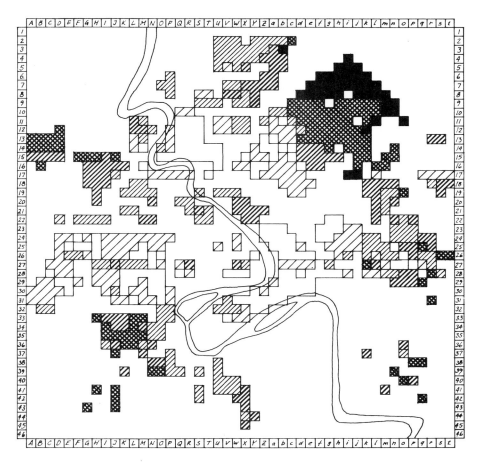

Fig. 2.5 Housing stress (0.5 km grid)

☐   score less than 251

▨   251–280

▨   281–330

▨   331–380

▨   381–430

■   more than 430

and degrees of stress in the existing residential areas of the city. However, exactly the same procedure can be used to analyse the potential of different urban areas for development or redevelopment.

In this case the grid squares of principal interest are those which cover unused land and land whose use can be changed or intensified. For housing the indicators would include such items as:

> present land ownership;
> land values;
> accessibility to existing services and amenities with potential for more intensive use;
> cost of providing new infrastructure or extending the existing etc.

Most of the indicator scores would be determined by the cost and technical thresholds of development for housing. It may be easier to include the respective weighting factors at this stage as for most indicators they are less likely to rest upon subjective value systems.

The resulting Potential Surface Map would show those areas suitable for housing development ranked by their suitability and ease of development.

References

Nottinghamshire—Derbyshire sub-regional Study-Papers from the Seminar on the Process of the Study, Centre for Environmental Studies, Information Paper II, London 1970.

KEEBLE, L., Principles and Practice of Town and Country Planning, *Estates Gazette*, London 1969.

MCHARG, I., *Design with Nature*, Doubleday, New York 1971.

ESTIMATING HOUSING NEED

2

A method for determining existing and projecting future household sizes and the requirements for dwelling units.

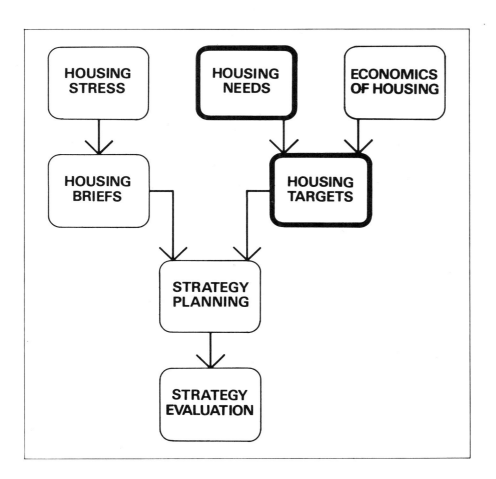

In order to assess the magnitude of the problem of urban housing provision, one has to determine:

(a) How many dwellings are needed at the present time to overcome the existing shortage? For this, the size of 'the existing suitable housing stock' needs to be taken.

(b) Over the next (say) 20 years, how many of the existing dwellings will have to be replaced because they are deteriorating? This is expressed by the 'rate of obsolescence'.

(c) How many new housing units will have to be built over the next (say) 20 years to cater for the expected growth of the city? That is, 'future housing needs'.

(d) What type of housing will be demanded by various groups of users in terms of its cost, size and service standards? That will establish 'housing targets'.

Existing need

This information is usually obtained by means of a survey of the existing housing stock. Such a survey would have to indicate:

(i) the total number of existing housing units; and
(ii) the number or proportion of the existing stock that is 'unsuitable' by definition.

By subtracting the number of unsuitable dwellings from the total housing units, the existing 'suitable' housing stock can be obtained. If this is compared with the existing number of households, the existing housing need can be established. For most cities this information can be obtained from existing census data. In the absence of such information, or where the definitions used in the census are disputed, it would be necessary to institute a survey for the purpose.

Replacement need

If the form of construction of the existing housing stock is known, the life span of the units can be ascertained. On the assumption that the present units have been erected at a steady rate over the preceding years, it can be assumed that the oldest houses would need replacing this year, while those built this year will need replacing at the end of their life. Thus if the average life span was, say, 25 years this would mean that the total housing stock would have to be replaced over 25 years . . . or, at a rate of 4% of the existing stock per year. Similarly, a life span of 30 years would give a replacement rate of 3.3% per annum, and of 50 years, 2%. Obviously if more information is available about the age and type of construction, a more accurate rate could be determined. This is necessary where the form of construction is not uniform over the city, or where the city has been built in two or more peaks of activity rather than steadily over the preceding years.

Future housing needs

Essentially this consists of estimating the number of additional households there will be in the city at a given date in the future. A crude way of doing this is to estimate the future population of the city and divide it by the expected household size at that date. More sophisticated methods are employed by demographers in their projections. As with all projections there is a danger of being off the mark, particularly if the base data is unreliable or inadequate, or if the projections are being made too far ahead in time. Yet the degree of accuracy required in forecasting housing needs is not very high. An indication of the 'order of magnitude' will suffice in most cases. For a start, it is enough to obtain the total number of housing units needed between now and some future date by adding the future housing need to the number have to be replaced and the number necessary to fulfil the existing housing need. By making this calculation for a few key dates, it is possible to draw a graph from which the total number of housing units needed at any particular date can be ascertained (Fig. 2.6).

Housing targets

The estimates of future housing needs can be qualified to obtain more specific targets for housing production. For example, the total housing need projections for each reference date can be broken down by

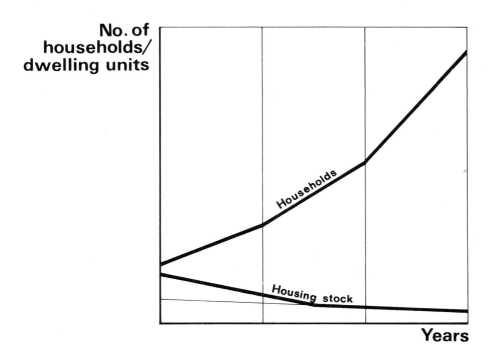

Fig. 2.6

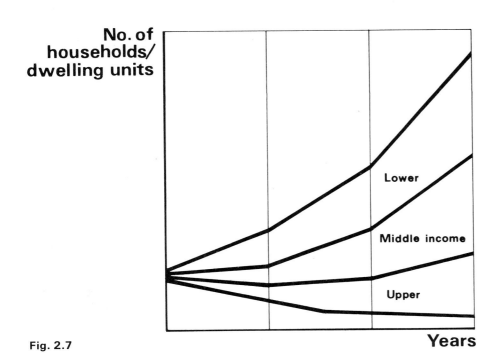

Fig. 2.7

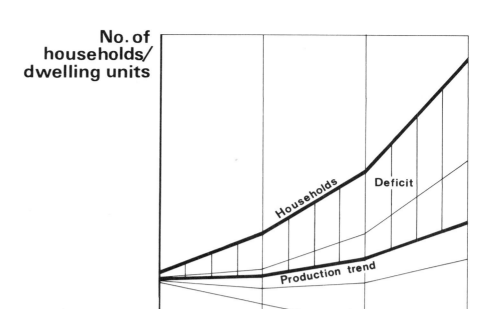

No. of households/dwelling units

Households

Deficit

Production trend

Years

Fig. 2.8

thresholds of cost related to the anticipated size of different urban income groups. This would entail projecting the distribution of the urban households by their ability to pay for housing (see Paper 3).

With the availability of more information, it becomes possible to sophisticate the target figures by anticipating the production trends in the private sector and therefore ascertain the necessary public sector response (Fig. 2.8).

A method for estimating future housing need

As mentioned above, the future housing need can be estimated in a number of ways, and over the years different methods have been established in different countries. The method described below allows fairly accurate predictions to be made for future housing needs in developing countries over a 20-year period. It has the advantage of being comparatively quick and simple, as well as demonstrating the implications of various assumptions.

Concept of household formations

A household may be simply defined as being that group of people, related or not who live and eat together. In most urban areas it can be assumed that the household is formed around the 'household manager', that is, the person responsible for the preparation of meals. In most instances, this person would be a female. The earliest age at which a female may begin to perform this role in her own right is usually the age of marriage (20–25) when she sets up her own home. She continues to perform this function until she 'retires' (50–55) after which she is usually incorporated into the household of a son or daughter. Therefore, the total number of households could be said to equal roughly the number of females between the ages of 20 and 55. There will be some women who marry and start a household earlier or later, and there will be some who are assimilated into the household of a younger woman before or after reaching the average 'retiring age'. Proportionately, the numbers involved are insignificant, and will, in most cases, cancel each other out. The advantage of using the 'household manager' as an indicator of household numbers (rather than the legal, male term) is that the age of marriage is fairly narrowly defined for women by social mores, whereas there is a greater spread in the corresponding age for males, since it it more often dependent on economic and educational considerations. Furthermore it also overcomes the problem of the dual household that is often maintained in developing countries; one rural and another urban.

In order to estimate future housing needs:

Method (see Fig. 2.9)

(1) Plot the figures for the total population and for women (20–55) for each census year in the respective graphs.
(2) Fill in the Household graph using either Average Household Size or Total Households, whichever information is available, corresponding to each reference date on the Poppulation graph.

(3) Drop a vertical line from each point in the Household Size graph to intersect a horizontal line projected from the corresponding point of the Women graph. The intersection of these two lines indicates the ratio of women (20–55) to household.
(4) Establish the trend (or trends) of future ratio of women/household. If this ratio is 'one', it indicates that there are no men (either single or whose wives are elsewhere) who form independent households. If the ratio is more than one, it indicates that there is a high proportion of extended households, or of unmarried women.
    You have to decide on the basis of your knowledge whether past trends are likely to continue or not. Different lines should be used for different assumptions.
(5) Establish the trend (or trends) of future average household size. Again, several different assumptions regarding changes in average household size should be tried.
(6) To make a projection for any given year, project the number of women (20–55) to that year. This can be done graphically, by cohort survival, matrices or any other method of demographic projection.
(7) Join the projected point by a horizontal line to the trend established in instruction 4 above.
(8) From the intersection draw a vertical line to obtain total number of dwellings needed.
(9) If desired, the vertical line from the Women/Household graph can be extended to intersect the trend in change of average household size.
(10) If a horizontal line is drawn from this intersection to the Population graph, then the intersection with the year line will indicate the total population at that date.

The total number of new housing units needed between now and the future date is given by subtracting from the figure obtained in 8 above, the existing usable stock, and then adding to it the number that have to be replaced due to obsolescence.

Example

Problem: To estimate the total number of households and the total population in the city in 1991.

Data:	1951	1971 (census year)
Total population	2.15	4.25 million
Total women (20–55)	312	722 thousands
Average household size	5.5	5.0
Total households	390	850 thousands

The above census data was plotted on to the relevant graphs (see Fig. 2.4). The intersection of the vertical line from the total number of households in 1951 and 1971 with the corresponding horizontal lines from the Women graph gave the ratios of women per household. This was 0.8 in 1951 and 0.85 in 1971.

By using a survivorship rate (i.e. combining migration with death rates) based on the previous rate, the women in the 20–55 cohorts were then projected by the cohort survival method over a 20-year period, thus giving the total female (20–55) population in 1991. All the women that will form this group in 1991 have already been born. Therefore fertility rates (the most volatile factor in population projections) do not enter the calculations. Also any cohorts outside the 20–55 range need not be considered since they do not significantly influence the number of households.

By looking at the historical and sociological situation in 1951 and 1971 a trend was observed for fewer single men to migrate to the city than previously. It was therefore assumed that the ratio of women/household which had increased from 0.8 in 1951 and to 0.85 in 1971 would increase to 0.9 in 1991. The next step was to draw a horizontal line from the total number of women (20–55) in 1991, which was 1.63 million and to intersect it with the 0.9 ratio line: in other words midway between the 0.8 and the 1.0 line.

Again an examination of past trends indicated a tendency for the average size of households to reduce over time. It was therefore assumed that in 1991 the average household would be 4.7 persons. The vertical line giving the total households was therefore extended till it intersected the average household size of 4.7. From this intersection, a horizontal line was drawn to meet the vertical 1991 year line. Along this horizontal line could then be read off the total population in 1991 as approximately 8.5 million.

References

1. BOGUE, DONALD J., *Principles of Demography*, John Wiley & Sons Inc., 1969.
2. CULLINGWORTH, J. B., *Housing Needs and Planning Policy*, Routledge & Kegan Paul, London 1966.
3. WALKDEN, A. H., The Estimation for the future numbers of private households in England and Wales. *Population Studies* XV (Nov. 1961) London School of Economics.
4. *Methods of Estimating Housing Needs*, United Nations No. 67 XVII 15.
5. ANGENOT, L. J. H., Age structure and the number of dwellings in the Netherlands.

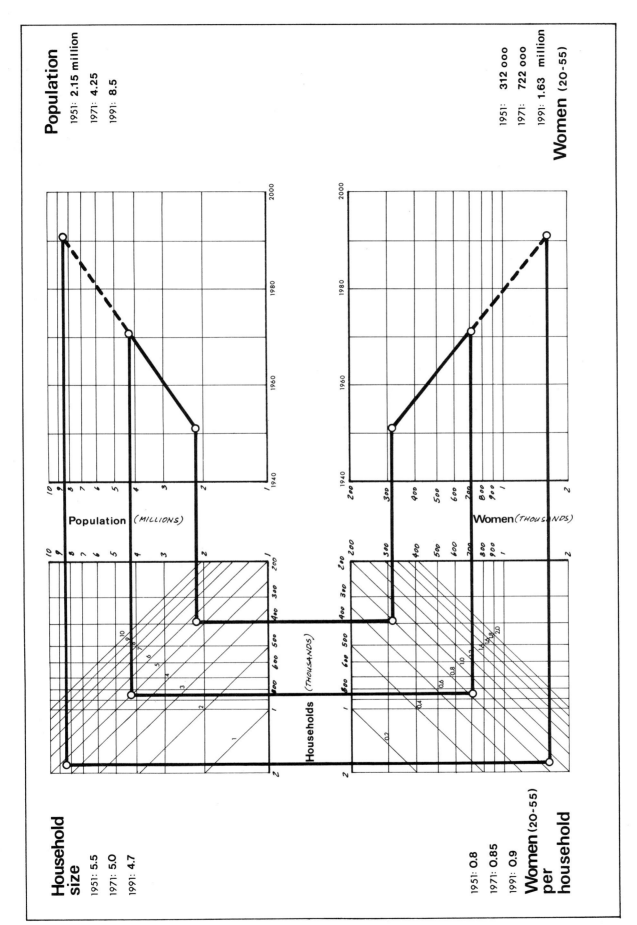

Population

1951: **2.15 million**

1971: **4.25**

1991: **8.5**

Women (20-55)

1951: **312 ooo**

1971: **722 ooo**

1991: **1.63 million**

Population (MILLIONS)

Women (THOUSANDS)

Households (THOUSANDS)

Households

Household size

1951: **5.5**

1971: **5.0**

1991: **4.7**

Women (20-55) **per household**

1951: **0.8**

1971: **0.85**

1991: **0.9**

Fig. 2.9

61

Proceedings of the World Population Conference 1965, U.N. No. 66 XIII 8 Vol. IV.

6. EVERSLEY, D. & JACKSON, J. N., Problems encountered in forecasting housing demand in an area of high economic activity. *Proceedings of the World Population Conference 1965.*

7. CANFIELD, G., *An Alternative Method of Projecting the Number and Size of Households.* TPI Journal, June 1970.

8. JOACHIM, M. E., *A Model for Estimating and Projecting the Housing Demand of an Urban Area in Ceylon*, Dissertation at the Edinburgh University.

THE ECONOMICS OF HOUSING

3

A technique for combining the principal components of capital cost, household income and conditions of repayment (rent) in order to establish 'abilities to pay' for urban housing.

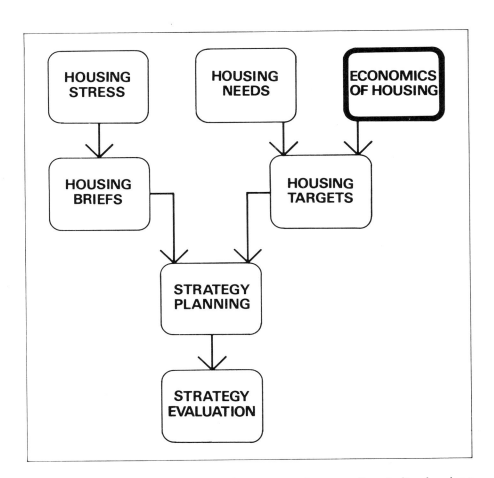

The three parameters of the housing economics equation, in its simplest form, are:

C = the initial capital cost of the asset
I = total annual household income
R = annual economic rent

The purpose of these notes is to define each of these parameters, to show how they are affected by social, economic and technical factors and, more important, how they interact. The argument is set in a theoretical framework, although it is based on numerous observations of real situations with particular reference to the problems of developing countries.

The nature of the relationships, which is treated in a generalized way in the body of the notes, is illustrated in the Appendix in the form of a fully worked out, although imaginary, example.

Capital cost

The first parameter is C. It represents the initial, once-for-all payment, whether it is determined freely by the market or conditioned by particular economic and social policies, to cover:

> the land on which the dwelling is to be erected, inclusive of all fees related to its acquisition or transfer (registration, taxes, duties, professional services, agents, etc.);
> the building itself;
> the fees of designers and supervisors (if applicable);
> the connections to service networks: electricity, water, sewage, gas, etc. (if applicable).

These will be examined separately below.

Any consideration of C must be meaningfully related to some notional standard, i.e. a norm expressing the amount of goods or services to be provided in relation to a consumer unit. In the particular context of housing, the basic consumer unit to which C relates is the individual household, even in the case of multi-family accommodation. In fact, the notions of dwelling and household are often inseparable, as for instance when households are defined for census purposes as people sharing the whole or part of a dwelling.

Dwelling standards, in a given society for a given socio-economic group at a given place and at a given point in time, are generally related to the size of household (N = number of people in household) either in a crude form (so many persons per inhabitable room, so much floor area per person, etc.) or in more sophisticated variants, for instance taking into account the age of the different members of household, their sex, their kinship, etc.

But whatever independent parameters are used to define standards, it will be found that the capital cost C will be composed of a part which is independent of such parameters, and a part that varies with them, mostly, although not necessarily, in linear fashion. In its most generalized formulation, C can be shown to vary approximately as shown in Fig. 2.10.

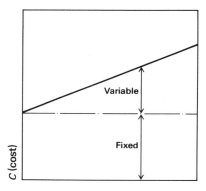

Fig. 2.10

The cost of land depends on the area required and the cost per unit of area. But the area of land required per dwelling is neither directly proportional to N nor completely fixed. In the case of individual dwellings on individual plots, it could be reasonably assumed that larger households requiring larger dwellings would be assigned larger plots; in the case of collective dwellings the allocation of land costs among dwellings is inevitably arbitrary, but could be made to reflect the relative cost of dwellings.

It is not proposed to consider here the issue of the unit cost of land and of the factors affecting it. For the purpose of the present exercise, this is taken to be an independent variable, in the same category as building wages, building materials costs, contractor's profits, household sizes or incomes.

The main factors affecting the cost of the building proper are:

    (1)   The quantity and unit price of materials and components: these in turn are affected by the type of building, by the standard of quality, by the technology used, by the dependence on imports, etc.

    (2)   The wages and productivity of building labour: these are affected by the technology used, by the degree of mechanization, by the skills required, by social overheads, etc.

    (3)   The contractor's overheads and profits, which are generally affected by their efficiency, by market conditions or, in the case of centrally planned economies, by national or local norms.

    (4)   Taxation and finance, which are conditioned by Government policies and by market conditions.

For a given standard, the costs of materials and wages grow with the area of the dwelling but not in direct proportion, whereas contractor's overheads and tax tend to be more closely related to the subtotal of materials and labour cost.

The non-proportionality of materials and labour costs is due to a variety of factors. Thus for instance an extra room normally requires only two or three additional walls and additional door, window, electrical points, etc., the latter being to a large extent independent of the room area; an extension to a roof may not require additional chimneys, ridge, eaves, rainwater pipes, etc.; additional appliances may be fed from the same central installation: tank, meter, cistern, etc.

Not only are materials not proportional to area, but the work content (for instance, expressed in man-hours) is not proportional to the amount of materials. This is because certain time-consuming operations such as setting out, starting off, scaffolding, tooling, etc. are unique, one-off events and their cost is to a large extent independent of the amount of materials consumed. This, incidentally, is the main limitation of estimates based on the so-called 'bills of quantities' which in a majority of cases assume fixed unit prices and therefore rigorous proportionality between quantities and prices.

Land

Building

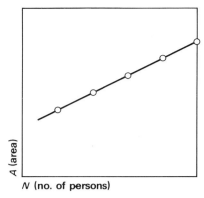

Fig. 2.11

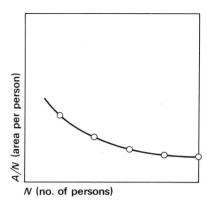

Fig. 2.12

But the area itself is not proportional to the size of household, because whatever the standard adopted, a minimum amount of facilities is required even for a one-person dwelling: kitchen, W.C., independent access, etc.

It is therefore reasonable to assume that, for a given standard, the area required for households of different sizes could be expressed as a linear function of the number of people as shown in Fig. 2.11. It follows that the area per person would be represented by a curve as shown in Fig. 2.12.

But since, as shown above, building cost itself is not proportional to area, its relationship is likely to take the form shown in Fig. 2.13; the cost per unit of floor area will therefore be variable as shown in Fig. 2.14.

Fees

Design fees tend to be roughly proportional to C, although here again in the majority of cases the fee, as a percentage of the cost of the building, tends to decrease with the cost.

Connection to mains

These can be taken to be practically independent of the size of the dwelling and therefore of the size of household.

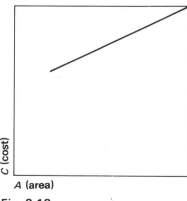

Fig. 2.13

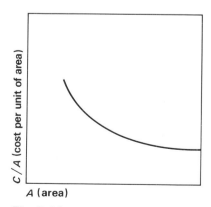

Fig. 2.14

If all the factors enumerated above are taken into account, it should be possible to express C as a simple function as follows: Total cost

$$C = (K + aA + br)(1 + \alpha) \qquad \text{Eqn 1}$$

where
$K =$ the fixed element of total cost
$a =$ marginal cost per unit of floor area, i.e. the cost of each additional unit of floor area
$A =$ floor area (m^2, ft^2, etc.)
$b =$ additional cost per bedroom
$r =$ number of bedrooms
$\alpha =$ a factor representing those elements of the total cost which are proportional to the building cost

It has already been noted that for a given standard the area of the dwelling A can be related to the number of people N; this can therefore be expressed as follows:

$$A = c + dN \qquad \text{Eqn 2}$$

where
$c =$ the floor area required for the minimum facilities common to all dwellings whatever the size of the household
$d =$ additional area required for each person in the household.

The number of bedrooms 'r' can also be expressed as a function of the number of people; thus, for instance, in many countries it is customary to express accommodation standards in terms of maximum number of persons per bedroom.

Therefore:

$$r = eN \qquad \text{Eqn 3}$$

where
$e =$ number of bedrooms per person

If the values of 'A' and 'r' are substituted in Eqn 1 the following expression relating total cost to size of household can be derived:

$$C = (K_1 + K_2 N)(1 + \alpha) \qquad \text{Eqn 4}$$

where
$K_1 = K + ac$
$K_2 = ad + be$

If all these factors are taken into account it will be obvious that C is related to N in the form shown in Figs 2.15 and 2.16.

The procedure to be followed to obtain the values of the coefficients is illustrated in the example provided in the Appendix.

The total annual household income I is the second major parameter to Income

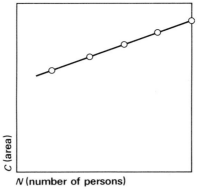

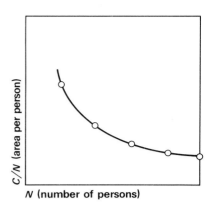

Fig. 2.15   Fig. 2.16

be considered. Depending on the social and economic system, it can be taken to include all the incomes entering into the household, including revenue in kind at its imputed value, but excluding direct taxation. It should also include subsidies, family allowances and other social benefits, if applicable.

The most general feature of household incomes is the inequality of their distribution among individual households. In practically all societies some households command greater incomes than others, with the consequence that a small proportion of households accounts for a large proportion of incomes and vice versa.

Income redistribution is among the principal objectives of social and economic development policies. Given that one of the most blatant forms of social injustice is inequality in real incomes, for instance through unemployment, the main issue can be how to reconcile growth with justice; housing policies can play an important role in such strategies.

Taking the individual household as the basic unit of housing needs or demand and the size of household (expressed in number of persons per household N) as its most salient feature, the first essential step consists of ascertaining (or forecasting, as the case may be) the percentage distribution of households of a given size falling within a given income bracket.

A convenient way of representing the relationship between household size and household income is a histogram as shown in Fig. 2.17. The vertical axis represents the percentage of households of a given size falling in each of the income brackets represented along the horizontal axis.

It should be noted that this representation is meaningful only if the income intervals marked along the horizontal axis are equal. In such a case, the histograms will reveal at a glance the most frequent income range and the order of magnitude of the inequalities of distribution of income among households of a given size.

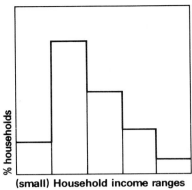
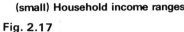

(small) Household income ranges

Fig. 2.17

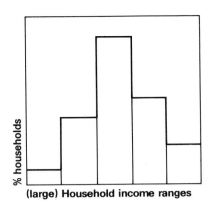

(large) Household income ranges

Fig. 2.18

In most countries, and in particular in the developing countries average household income tends to grow with household size, especially when the household comprises more than one wage earner. If this is the case, the histogram of income distribution of larger households will look like Fig. 2.18 where it will be noted that the peak of the distribution has been shifted towards a higher income range.

When income ranges as collected in socio-economic surveys are not equal and, in general, to facilitate comparisons between income distributions of households of different sizes, it is often more convenient to adopt a different representation such as shown in Fig. 2.19, where the cumulative percentage of households of a given size with an income less than a given amount is plotted on a vertical axis. This representation has the further advantage of enabling linear interpolation between fixed income ranges.

An alternative representation of the same phenomenon is the one known as the 'Lorenz curve' as shown in Fig. 2.20. In a Lorenz curve, the households are first ranked in ascending order of income and the cumulative percentage of households is plotted against the cumulative percentage of total income they account for.

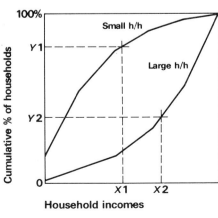

Fig. 2.19

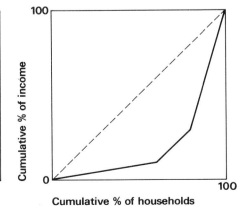

Fig. 2.20

The more uneven the distribution of income among households, the more the Lorenz curve will depart from a straight diagonal line. This departure can be expressed as the ratio of the area between the diagonal and the Lorenz curve, on the one hand, and the area of half the square, on the other. If incomes were evenly distributed among all households, this ratio would be 0.

As will be seen later the share of income devoted to housing tends to vary among households of different sizes and different incomes. In general, however, it has been observed that this share is higher for the lower incomes in most societies; this is particularly the case of the urban populations in developing countries.

Economic rent

The economic rent R is the third parameter in the housing economics equation. It can be defined as the total sum of recurrent payments (for instance on an annual basis) necessary to cover the initial cost of the asset and its preservation in working or acceptable conditions. It therefore comprises the following four elements:

(1) the amortization of the initial capital cost;
(2) the interest on such capital;
(3) the cost of current repairs and maintenance;
(4) the cost of management.

Amortization

This is the notional amount which should be set aside, say every year, to replace the initial value of the asset at the end of its useful or expected life. As such it can be expressed as a percentage of C and it can be calculated in several arbitrary ways; for instance, it can be assumed that the asset depreciates at a constant rate, in which case the same amount of amortization will be required every year.

Alternatively it could be assumed that the rate of depreciation is higher at the beginning of the life of the asset and lower towards the end. Whatever the method of calculation, it is obvious that amortization payments will be greater the higher the initial cost and smaller the longer the expected life of the asset.

To be precise, the amount to be set aside for amortization should also take into account the residual value of the asset at the end of its useful or expected life, and if the asset has to be demolished, the cost of such demolition.

Interest

The interest to be paid on capital represents the remuneration of that capital in traditional economic theory. In a market economy, the current interest rate is determined by the complex interplay of market factors and it tends to approximate the average yield of investment, or the opportunity cost of such investment in the case where it is not possible to assign a market value to the yield of a social investment.

It is important to note that the interest should be calculated not only on the monies borrowed (in which case it will be fixed by the lender, be it a bank, a public agency or a private financier) but also on the monies contributed by the owner occupier, on the basis of the yield that such capital would have produced had it been invested in an alternative asset.

In general the prevailing interest rate is related to the risk of the investment: lower risk investments usually carry lower interest rates than higher risk ones. It is also true that in developing countries current interest rates are higher than in industrialized countries because of the general scarcity of domestic capital available for productive or social investment.

Prevailing interest rates, especially for long term loans such as those applying to housing, are also influenced by the rate of inflation: the longer the loan, the more the repayments will be affected by the inflation of the current prices of goods and services.

It is common to combine amortization and interest on housing loans into a single value which remains constant over the period of the payment. This amount, expressed as a percentage of the initial cost, is of course

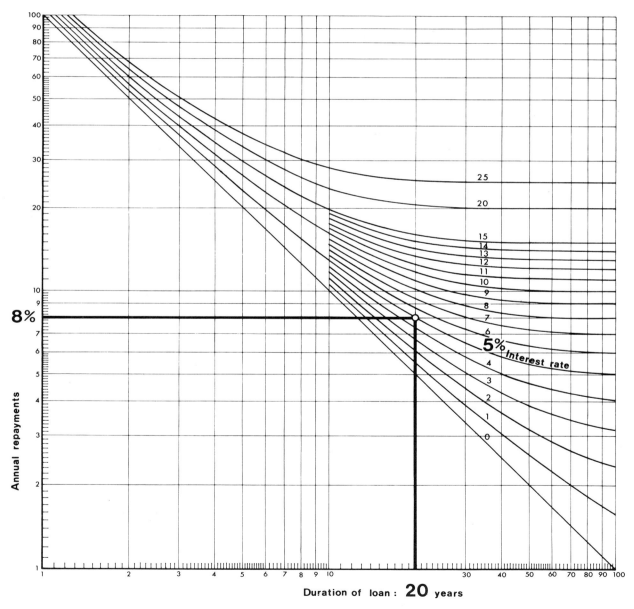

Fig. 2.21

dependent on the number of years over which the amortization is calculated and on the interest rate, as shown in Fig. 2.21. Each regular payment comprises a different proportion of amortization and interest, the former increasing and the latter decreasing with time.

Maintenance and repairs

Any asset, however durable, requires a certain amount of maintenance and repairs over its useful life. Some of these operations are of a recurrent nature and therefore can be predicted in advance; others have to be performed when the need arises. An example of the former is painting of joinery and interior decoration or, in the case of traditional mud construction, plastering after the rainy season; an example of the latter is the replacement of light bulbs when they are burnt out, or of tap washers when they leak or the clearing of drains when they are obstructed.

Over long periods of time both types of operation tend to follow a regular pattern and average out to an amount which is only slightly affected by the age of the asset. However the nature of maintenance and repairs is such that that they cannot be postponed without seriously impairing the performance or durability of the building and its parts.

Standards of maintenance and repair vary considerably between countries, between types of building, between forms of tenure, between individual households. But for a given accepted standard, maintenance and repairs are related to the initial quality of the parts of the building: it is therefore possible to find different combinations of initial high quality and low maintenance or low quality and high maintenance.

In the last resort both the initial cost and the future maintenance cost of each part of the building, and therefore of the building as a whole, should be combined in a single value usually referred to as 'cost-in-use' consisting of the initial cost converted in its equivalent annual value (according to the parameters in Table 1 above) and of the annual maintenance cost.

The monetary value of maintenance and repair operations can be reduced to the extent to which some of these are carried out by the occupant himself. This applies in particular to owner occupation and, in developing countries, to people exposed to seasonal unemployment or to cronic underemployment. It can be said that one of the major incentives to providing dwellings for owner occupation, second to the encouragement of personal saving, is the reduction of the commitment of the landlord to current maintenance and repairs.

Management

The expenses involved in managing a given stock of dwellings occur only when these dwellings are rented. These expenses, all too often neglected in estimates of public housing programmes, can be of a higher order of magnitude than that of current maintenance.

The three main basic ratios

Having defined the three parameters of the equation: C, I and R, it is possible to bring them together in the form of three two-by-two ratios as shown in Fig. 2.22.

72

By definition the ratios are non-dimensional which means that com-

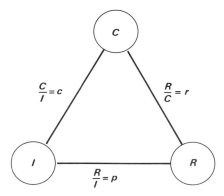

Fig. 2.22

parisons between countries become possible, having eliminated the problems inherent in the use of official or arbitrary rates of exchange between national currencies.

The three ratios are as follows:

$$\frac{C}{I} = c = \text{initial cost of the asset in years of annual income of household}$$

$$\frac{R}{C} = r = \text{annual economic rent as a percentage of capital cost}$$

$$\frac{R}{I} = p = \text{share of annual income devoted to rent.}$$

Since there are only three parameters, if two of the ratios are known, the third ratio is determined. This means that the three ratios are interdependent as shown below:

$$c \times r = \frac{C}{I} \times \frac{R}{C} = \frac{R}{I} = \quad p = c \times r \qquad \text{Eqn 5}$$

Representative values of this relationship are illustrated in Fig. 2.23.

It has been shown that the initial capital cost of the dwelling varies, among others, with the size of the household. Since households have different sizes, amenity, space and quality standards adopted for a given situation, it follows that 'average' costs of dwelling are to a large extent meaningless.

The floor area per person decreases with the size of household (Fig. 2.12), the cost per unit of floor area decreases with the size of dwelling (Fig. 2.14) and, more generally, the cost per person decreases with the size of household (Fig. 2.16). Standards or norms specifying any of these variables in terms of average values are therefore of limited use in the formulation and implementation of housing policies.

It has also been shown that incomes tend to be unevenly distributed between households of different sizes and within a given household

Summing up

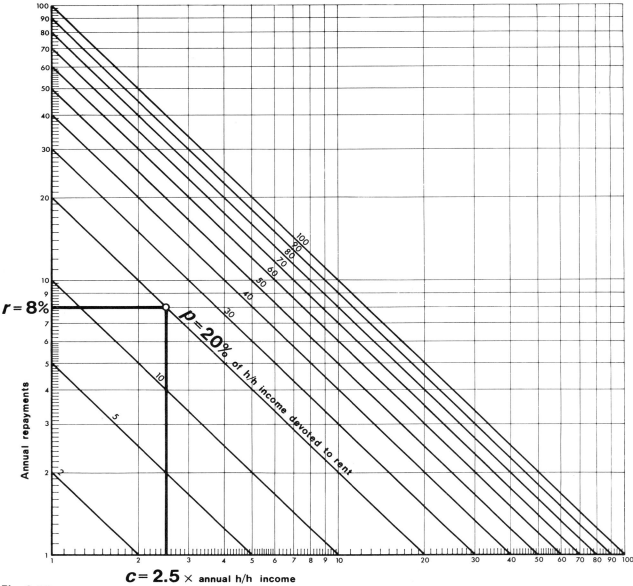

Annual repayments

$r = 8\%$

$P = 20\%$ of h/h income devoted to rent

$c = 2.5 \times$ annual h/h income

Fig. 2.23

size. The actual shape of the distribution varies, but in general average income per head tends to be smaller for larger households. Again, the formulation of housing policies in terms of average household income is largely meaningless.

Furthermore, there is a discrepancy between housing needs or expectations (in so far as they are reflected in housing standards) and household incomes. Some large families requiring larger accommodation have very low incomes in any society; conversely, some small households command high incomes. This diversity should be reflected in the setting of housing targets.

It has further been shown that the annual economic rent is conditioned by factors largely, if not totally, outside the range of responsibility of designers and planners. Rates of amortization and of interest on capital, management costs, and, to a lesser extent, maintenance and repair costs, are determined by the general economic and social conditions of society and can be altered only by deliberate interventions which, whatever their actual form amount to a direct or indirect subsidy, in other words some sort of redistribution of wealth.

When the three parameters are combined in a single relationship between the corresponding three ratios, it becomes apparent that the economic viablity of a housing programme is a function of reasonable or arbitrary values assigned to these ratios.

If the share of income devoted to rent 'p' is fixed as part of an overall social policy and the economic rent 'r' is dictated by the market, the ratio of the cost of the dwelling to annual income is limited; if this ratio is exceeded, households cannot afford the economic rent.

If on the other hand 'c' is determined by prevailing norms, by the current cost of inputs and by the relative productivity of house-building labour and 'r' is fixed as above, 'p' may turn out to be in excess of what the society or individual households are prepared to accept.

Finally, if 'p' and 'c' are fixed as above, it may turn out that the corresponding 'r' is too far below an acceptable rate of return on capital.

A housing policy must recognize these facts, especially the fundamental one of the inequalities between the ability (or willingness) to pay and the standard of accommodation that households of different sizes and incomes expect. In all societies, some households must be assisted financially by the society to fill the gap between what they consider essential and what they can afford; others can just about manage economically, but require other facilities (technical or legal assistance, appropriate tenure, convenient credit, etc.); others finally, usually a small minority in rapidly urbanizing areas in developing countries, do not require any assistance and can be supplied by the market. Any realistic housing programme must reflect this diversity.

Let us assume that in a particular situation it has been calculated that at a given time current acceptable housing standards require that households of different sizes should have at their disposal the following floor spaces and number of bedrooms:

Appendix

Example

	N (h/h–size)	A (area)	r (no. of bedrooms)
(1)	1–2	40	1
(2)	3–4	55	2
(3)	5–6	70	3
(4)	7–8	85	4
(5)	9–10	100	5

It has been shown in section 2.5 that the total initial capital cost of the dwelling can be expressed as a function of its area and number of bedrooms:

$$C = (K + aA + br)(1 = \alpha)$$

To apply the above space standards to this equation a number of cost assumptions have to be made.

The fixed element of total cost (K), i.e. central installation, connection to mains etc., is assumed to amount to 400 US \$*. The cost of each additional unit of floor space (a) is estimated as \$12 per square metre and the additional cost per bedroom (b) is taken as \$120. The costs proportional to the building cost, such as overheads, tax and fees are estimated as 10% ($\alpha = 0.1$) in this example. The initial capital cost (C) can then be established for various dwelling sizes:

$$(K \quad + \quad aA + \quad br)(1 + \alpha) = C$$

(1)	$(400 + 480 + 120) \times 1.1$	$= 1100$
(2)	$(400 + 660 + 240) \times 1.1$	$= 1430$
(3)	$(400 + 840 + 360) \times 1.1$	$= 1760$
(4)	$(400 + 1020 + 480) \times 1.1$	$= 2090$
(5)	$(400 + 1200 + 600) \times 1.1$	$= 2420$

Alternatively the total initial capital cost can be expressed as a function of the number of people per household, as mentioned in the section on total cost (p. 00).

$$C = (K_1 + K_2 N)(1 + \alpha)$$

From the above table of space standards the floor area required for the minimum facilities common to all dwellings (C) works out to be 25 m². We can then establish the cost of the floor area (K_1) required for the minimum facilities:

$$K_1 = K + ac$$
$$K_1 = 400 + 12 \times 25 = 700$$

The additional area required for each person in the household (d) is given as 7.5 m² in our initial space standards. The additional cost per person (K_2) can be obtained from the following equation:

$$K_2 = ad + bc$$

where c is the number of bedrooms per person.

$$K_2 = 12 \times 7.5 + 120 \times 0.5$$
$$K_2 = 90 + 60 = 150$$

Using the same household size breakdown as before, the initial capital cost of the dwelling can be tabulated as follows:

$$(K_1 \quad + \quad K_2 N)(1 + \alpha) = C$$

(1)	$(700 + 300) \times 1.1$	$= 1100$
(2)	$(700 + 600) \times 1.1$	$= 1430$
(3)	$(700 + 900) \times 1.1$	$= 1760$

* Throughout this example, monetary values are expressed in US \$ for the sake of convenience; it should be appreciated that all calculations can be made in any national currency.

(4) $(700 + 1200) \times 1.1 = 2090$
(5) $(700 + 1500) \times 1.1 = 2420$

Let us assume further that the population to be housed is distributed by size of household and by ranges of incomes as shown in the table below.

Absolute number of households

Household sizes N	Income groups						Total
	200	200–400	400–600	600–800	800–1000	1000	
1–2	44	66	55	33	13	9	220
3–4	43	87	73	47	23	17	219
5–6	25	75	63	42	25	20	250
7–8	7	38	38	30	22	15	150
9–10	1	8	18	23	27	13	90
Total	120	274	247	175	110	74	1000

Percentage of each household size group

	200	200–400	400–600	600–800	800–1000	1000	Total
1–2	20	30	25	15	6	4	100
3–4	15	30	25	16	8	6	100
5–6	10	30	25	16	10	8	100
7–8	5	25	25	20	15	10	100
9–10	1	9	20	25	30	15	100
Total	12.0	27.4	24.7	17.5	11.0	7.4	100

Cumulative percentage of each household size group

	200	200–400	400–600	600–800	800–1000	1000
1–2	20	50	75	90	96	100
3–4	15	45	70	86	94	100
5–6	10	40	65	82	92	100
7–8	5	30	55	75	90	100
9–10	1	10	30	55	85	100
Total	12.0	39.4	64.1	81.6	92.6	100

Finally it is possible, to bring together in a single graph all parameters examined so far, including the crucial ratios defined in section 5 of the main note. This is in the form of a nomogram with four parts: **Nomogram**

A expresses the relationship between floor area and total cost
B represents the relationship between 'p', 'r' and 'c'
C represents the cumulative percentage of households of a given size earning less than a given income
D represents the percentage of households of a given size.

Assumption 1 (see Fig. 2.25)

The operation of the nomogram can be illustrated by one case drawn from the example presented in the appendix. Take a household of 5–6 people. They require 70 m² of floor area. Carrying this point on to graph A, it is possible to read the cost of such dwelling, namely $1760. Assume that a mortgage can be obtained over 20 years of 5% interest. Thus the current economic rent for this type of dwelling is 8% of the capital cost p.a. and the household cannot afford more than 24% of its annual income for rent. Figure 3.15 shows that under such conditions the dwelling should not cost more than 3 years of income.

Carrying the reading from *A* to *B* (Fig. 2.25) until it intersects the line corresponding to '*c*' = 3 and transferring this reading to *C* it will be possible to read the percentage of households in the 5–6 size group earning *less* than the corresponding income, namely 64%. This has been

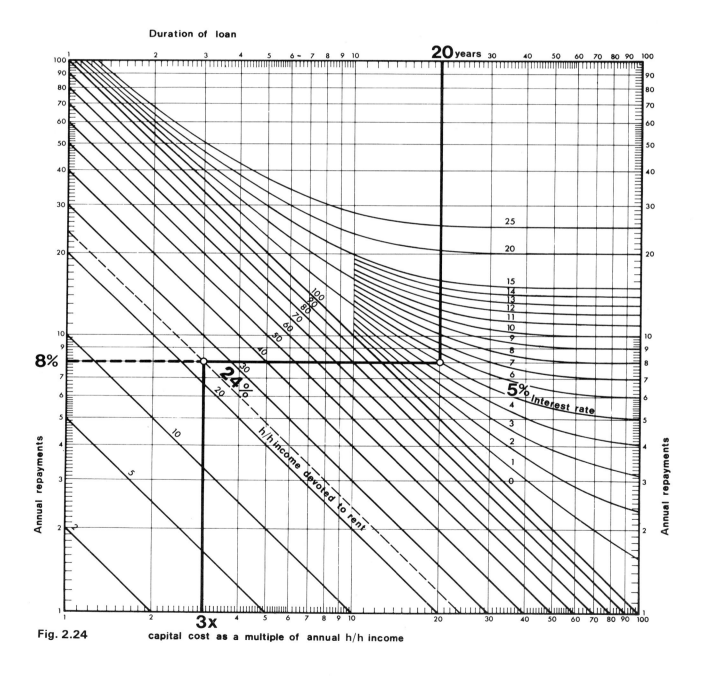

Fig. 2.24   capital cost as a multiple of annual h/h income

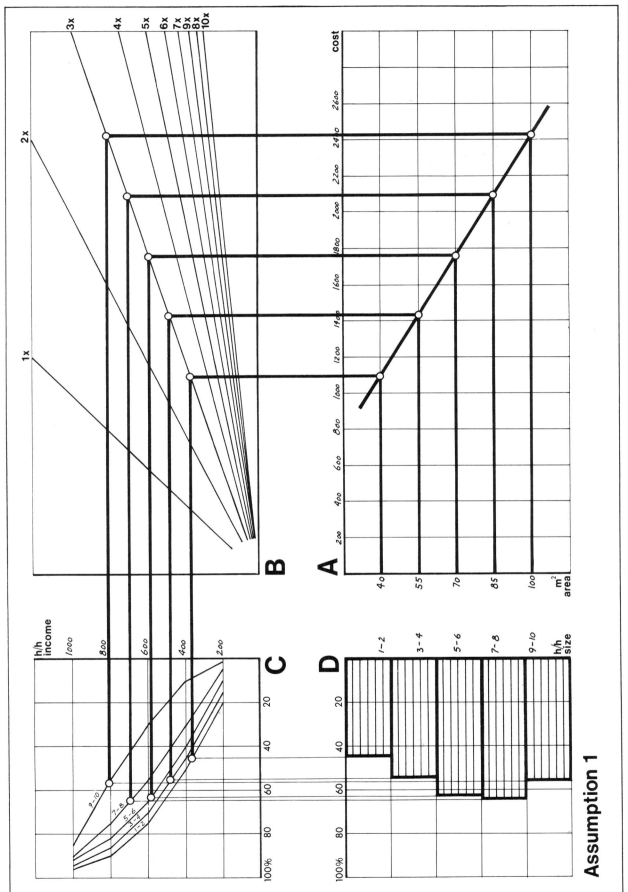

Assumption 1

Fig. 2.25

repeated for each household size group and the readings projected down to graph *D* where the shaded area indicates the percentage of households unable to afford a dwelling under the above mentioned assumptions.

Assumption 2 (see Fig. 2.26)

A Housing Authority is building dwellings intended for households with incomes between $200–500. Households in these income groups can spend no more than 20% (*p*) of their income on housing although the prevalent economic rent is only 5% (*r*) of the cost of the dwelling, which means that it will have to be financed over a 30-year period at a subsidized interest rate of 3%. The graph below shows that the construction of dwellings for this clientele cannot cost more than four times the annual household income.

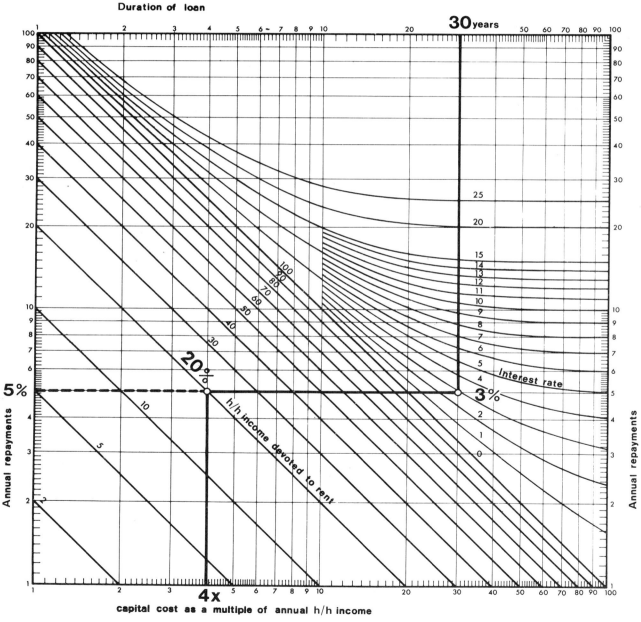

Fig. 2.26

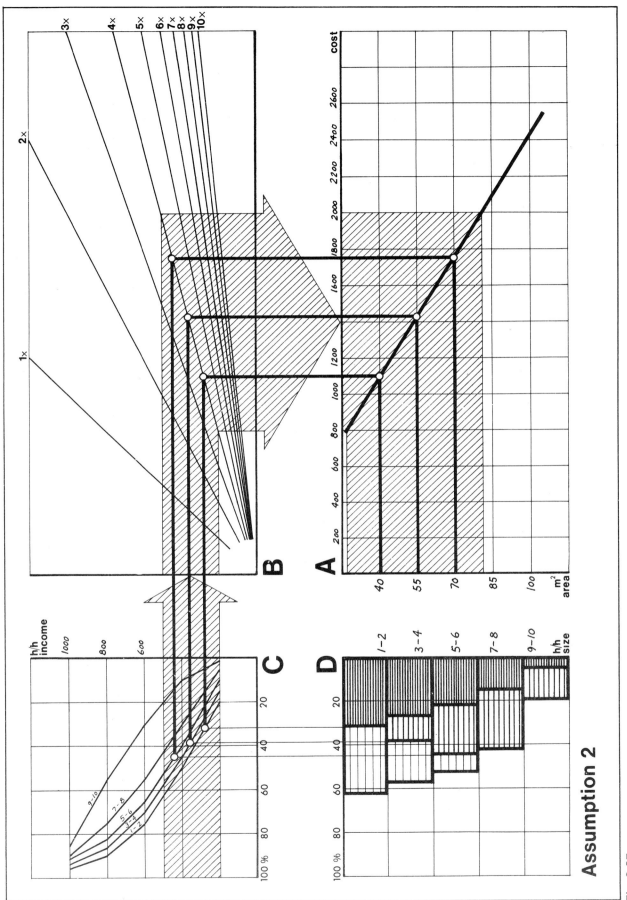

Assumption 2

Fig. 2.27

Thus by projecting the income ranges from graph C to the 'c' = 4 radial in B and on to the cost scale of graph A it can be seen that dwellings that can be afforded by this income group will cost between $800–2000. By continuing the projection in A the areas that can be provided range between 26–80 m². However, as stated above a minimal habitable dwelling for 1–2 people requires 40 m² of area costing $1 100. Thus by projecting these readings back from the area and cost scales of A it can be seen from graph C that all households with an income of less than $380 cannot afford minimal housing. Even those with an income of $500 cannot afford more than 80 m². Therefore with the standards adopted only three bedroomed houses can be provided. Thus all households of 7–10 persons who can afford housing at all will have to occupy them in conditions of overcrowding (more than two persons per bedroom).

Graph D shows, by projecting across from graph C, the distribution of the $200–500 income groups by household size. It shows the proportions of each group that cannot afford even a minimal one bedroom dwelling (dark hatch); and those who are able to afford 'standard' housing (light hatch).

HOUSING BRIEFS

4

A procedure for establishing for different 'client groups' the priorities of demand for housing and the preparation of performance specifications.

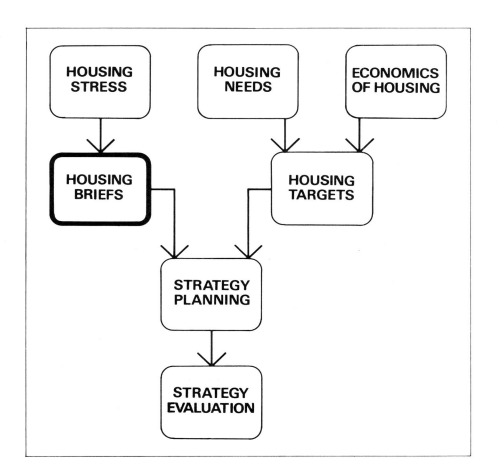

The theoretical basis of a 'client-oriented' approach to urban housing is: that professional or public intervention in housing provision is determined solely by the demands for housing of identified groups of users.

This premise means the reversal of approach adopted by nearly all public housing agencies. It means the reversal of a process whereby the resources available for housing are assessed; the numerical housing need is established; minimum standards are set and housing units are constructed with little, if any, recourse to the future users or present 'clients' of public housing. Such housing is occupied only because of the lack of alternative available to the user, created by the mismatch between supply and demand. In fact, throughout the world, examples exist where despite apparently vast housing defects, public housing is so inappropriate that it is left empty or has been occupied by households for whom it was not intended.

In a client-oriented approach, 'Client Groups' are identified by their common demands for housing. These demands are translated into 'Client's Briefs' and combined with the numerical needs of each group to produce a 'Design Brief'. The brief, therefore will be a description of the product both qualitatively and in terms of the quantity to be provided. Whereas traditionally housing strategies have concentrated on reducing construction costs and minimizing space and amenity standards, a client orientated strategy is likely to centre round the design of alternative financial, legal and administrative systems that can make existing resources more responsive to the clients' briefs.

The reconnaissance survey of demographic data and projections together with a review of the city's range of household incomes will have given a broad indication of the urban income groups and their abilities to pay for housing. A combination of these with the prevalent housing production rate will have established the order of magnitude of new housing need by each income group. The residential area characteristics and housing stress maps will have established those areas of the city characterized by different types and degrees of housing stress. From this information areas of the city can be selected as those where potential 'clients' with definite though differing demands for housing can be found.

The next stage of the process is to interview householders living under different conditions of 'housing stress' in order to establish their own priorities of demand for housing. The process of analysing the interview data is the stage at which the different 'Client Groups' are identified and their predominant demands for housing are ranked. It is important to remember that some of the households interviewed not only represent client groups already in the city but also newcomers still to migrate from other towns and rural areas. In fact, the majority of new housing provisions in a city will often have to be for people who are not yet citizens.

In any data-gathering exercise there is a temptation to collect as much information as possible 'in case it comes in handy sometime'. This should be avoided not only because of the time it wastes, but also because information not directly pertinent to the problem has the danger of distracting attention from the central issues.

The table (pp. 86–87) is an outline check-list of the major components that are likely to be needed in the drafting of a client's brief. It is neither exhaustive nor conclusive but can be used as a guide. It is presented in the order of:
      (1) *Client's Brief* clauses
      (2) *correlation* of information:
            (i) to identify different client groups and to construct housing briefs for them;
           (ii) to update old statistics or to correct assumptions made in the analysis stage of the process;

(3) *Information* required direct from urban householders concerning their resources and demands for housing.

It is important, when setting out to design a household survey, to be clear about the objective of the survey which is the preparation of a brief for each client group. Therefore the Client's Brief column is presented first, in the table, though of course the columns will be used in the reverse order.

Each column is referenced to the one to the right of it to indicate the links and dependencies between the three stages.

Column 3 of the table lists the basic information that is required from householders in order to establish users' demands for housing and to correct assumptions made, or to update information used, in the Analysis stage of the reconnaissance survey.

Information from household survey (column 3)

Much of the information required concerns existing conditions of housing, services and amenities. Many of the key questions, however, concern householders priorities of demand for the change of existing conditions. These are the issues on which a 'Client oriented' housing brief can be written. But such priorities are inevitably dependent upon the experience of the people demanding them. Therefore it is essential not only to know what people say their demands are, but also to know the reasons for their demands. For example, two groups of people may have a high priority of demand for an improved supply of water; one because they do not have access to water at the moment; and the other because, though water is available, they have to pay a lot for it. An analysis of the reasons for the demand of a housing provision is essential for the formulation of a brief that can satisfy that demand.

This is one reason why the information necessary from householders includes a record, not only of what people want, but also of what they have, or do not have, at the moment. The other, equally important reason, is to feed the information back into an 'urban housing data bank'. As pointed out, the initial analysis stage of the reconnaissance survey has had to rely on 'second-hand' information, often collected for purposes other than the establishment of a client-oriented housing programme. Assumptions have been made in the absence of information. Obsolete statistics and irrelevant standards may have been used. The household survey is the first stage of the process of setting up a continuous feedback or monitoring mechanism which is essential for the smooth running of a continuous housing process. For instance, the survey may reveal that the household size of several groups differ from the average gleaned from a past census, thus radically changing the projections of housing need. Or it may demonstrate a different definition of 'habitable dwelling' than that officially used to describe the urban housing stock. This could fundamentally alter the figures of housing deficit and so on.

To carry out a household survey, interviewers are often employed to administer carefully prepared interview schedules. This procedure may save time in obtaining a large sample but is a poor substitute for planners themselves 'getting their feet muddy' by experiencing the

(1) Client's Brief (for each client group)	(2) Correlation	(3) Information
Dwelling size and domestic space	*Household*	
I Range of dwelling sizes (A, D, F)	A Range of h/h sizes (1 × frequency)	1 Occupants of each dwelling by sex, age, occupation, relation to h/holder
II Ground level/upper floor accommodation (D, F)		
III Space (room) relationships (E, F)	*Tenure*	
IV Private open space (E, F)	B Tenure patterns (h/holder) (2 × frequency—owner priv. tenant pub. tenant)	2 Tenure status of head of h/h (owner, public or private tenant) a—preferences of tenure type b—reasons for present tenure
V Privacy of dwelling and in dwelling (F)	C (Sub)tenure patterns (3 × frequency)	3 (Sub)tenants in dwelling a—desirability of (sub)tenants
	Domestic space	4 Number and area of rooms (a) priorities for change
	D Distribution of area per person (occupancy rate) (1 × 4 × 5 × frequency)	5 Types and area of private open space (incl. verandah) (a) priorities for change
	E Use of space by activities (6 × frequency)	6 Uses of rooms and private open space (incl. commerce) (a) shared use of space (b) desirability and priorities for change (c) demand for privacy
	F Demand for additional or different types of space (4 × 5 × 6 × 3 × frequency)	
Domestic services	*Domestic services*	7 Availability of water
VI Provision of services (individual/communal) (G)	G Availability and demand for improved services (7 × 8 × 9 × 10 × 11 × frequency)	8 Availability of drainage
		9 Availability of electricity
		10 Method of garbage disposal
		11 Priorities of demand for improved services (7, 8, 9, 10)
Public services	*Public services and location*	12 Location of daily shopping
VII Ease of access to services as walking time (distance) or transport time (H, I)	H Frequency of use of public services by location (12–17 × 18 × frequency)	13 Location of school
		14 Location of clinic
VIII Priorities of provision of services (H, I)	I Accessibility and priorities of change in access to public services (18 × 19 × 20 × frequency)	15 Location of cinema, etc.
		16 Location of recreation space
		17 Location of religious centre
Location	J Travel cost and time by location to place of work by means of transport (22 × 23 × frequency)	18 Frequency of use of service (12–17)
IX Location of housing relative to centres of employment, other urban centres, services (travel distances) (J, K)	K Priorities of location of h/h (20 × 21 × 24 × frequency)	19 Means of transport to services (12–17)
		20 Desirability and priorities for change in location of public services (12–17)
		21 Location of relatives often visited
		22 Location of place of work
		23 Means of transport to work (a) travel time (b) travel cost
		24 Desirability and priorities for change in location or means of transport to work
Technical intervention	*Technical recources*	
X Institutional provision of infrastructure (L)	L Availability of building skills in h/h by trades and availability of time	25 Availability of building skills (direct or by exchange of labour, no cash transfer)

(1) *Client's Brief* (for each client group)	(2) *Correlation*	(3) *Information*
XI Institutional provision of superstructure (L)	(25 × 26 × frequency)	(a) Bricklayer, Mason (b) Plasterer
XII Flexibility of growth of dwellings (D, E, F, L)		(c) Joiner (d) Roofer (e) Electrician (f) Plumber
XIII Popular provision of public services (school, recreation space, etc.) (L)		26 Time available for house construction

Limits of cost to household	*Financial resources*	
XIV Capital down-payment and repayment rates on (a) land and infrastructure (b) superstructure (Q, R, N)	M Income distribution by h/h size (1 × 29 × frequency) N H/h income distribution by source (27 × 28 × 29 × frequency) — H/h expenditure by h/h size (1 × 30–37 × frequency) P H/h expenditure by h/h income (30–37 × 29 × frequency) Q Ability to pay rent by h/h income by present rent R Ability to pay rent by h/h size by present rent (1 × 31 × 38 × frequency)	27 H/h occupants employed 28 H/h occupants in casual employment (self-employed) 29 Total h/h income (net) (a) income from non-employment sources (farm, village, relatives) (b) income from rent (see 3)
XV Local property taxes (a) capital payment on public services (b) maintenance charges (water rates etc.) (O, P) (O, P) (O, P)		30 H/h expenditure on food 31 H/h expenditure on rent 32 H/h expenditure on rates 33 H/h expenditure on water 34 H/h expenditure on electricity 35 H/h expenditure on others (a) clothing (b) transport (see 23, b) (c) travel (to village etc.) (d) fuel (e) education (f) entertainment 36 Remittance to village, relatives, etc. 37 H/h savings 38 Willingness to pay rent

XVI Statement of Dominant Problems	S Dominant problems (39 × frequency)	39 Dominant problem

conditions of their clients and discussing at first-hand their clients' demands and aspirations. Often the key insight into housing demand will come from informal doorstep conversations with potential clients and not from the coded answers to predetermined questions on an interview schedule. For this reason, the professionals who will later be responsible for drawing up housing briefs and for developing housing strategies must actively participate in the household surveys, even if they cannot cover the whole sample themselves.

Correlations of user demands (column 2)

The second column in the table is a list of correlations of information gleaned from the survey of user demands for housing (column 3). The overriding importance of this stage of survey analysis is to establish different client groups. The survey areas were selected from the Housing Stress and Residential Area Characteristic maps. Thus each survey will cover areas with similar conditions but this does not mean that all the occupants of each area have the same demands or expectations for housing. The analysis of survey data is therefore to synthesize the responses of a sample of individuals into a series of representative groups with common demands for housing—Client Groups.

The formation of client groups from correlations of the household survey data, must be done to some degree of detail. So in the first instance, there are likely to be many different briefs, one for each client group, distinguished from each other by perhaps only one or two criteria. This can best be described by the example of a simplified tree.

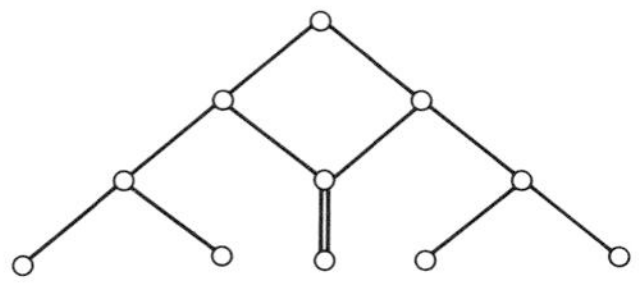

Ability to pay group

Locational demands

Demands for domestic services

Demands for domestic space

Fig. 2.28

For instance, within one income group there may emerge two distinct types of demand for the location of housing (say, one central and the other peripheral where limited agriculture can be pursued). Each of these groups may be divided into two further groups by the priorities of their demands for domestic services, though one of the 'central groups' have the same demands for services as one of the 'peripheral groups'. The consideration of demands for domestic space may reveal a further subdivision into five different client groups, and so on. The numerical strength of each group can only be gauged by their proportional representation in the sample of household interviews undertaken. Therefore, considerable care must be taken in the choice of sampling technique.

By the correlation of different data gleaned from household interviews, the survey analysis should also provide all the information needed in the preparation of the Clients' Briefs.

The correlation and presentation of numerical statistics is relatively simple. But to be useful in the identification of client groups and the formulation of briefs, the survey analysis must present less tangible data with equal clarity. For instance, (in item B) the presentation of preferences for different types of tenure is of equal, if not of more importance than the recording of existing tenure patterns. Similarly, it is essential to show what distribution of dwelling area per person is demanded by different households as well as what they have at present (item D).

There will be some information gained from the survey that cannot be analysed and presented in the form of histograms or graphs. Very often this is the sort of information most useful to brief formulation. It must therefore be presented with equal clarity though it may have to take the form of a report or written notes. No data should be withheld as the people who undertake the survey may not always be the same as those who prepare to use the client's brief.

Clients' brief (column 1)

The first column is a list of headings which should be included amongst the clauses of the brief for housing of each client group. Though in the table they are loosely combined under six headings when they are drawn up for each client group, it should be made clear which clauses of the brief are essential needs to meet the client's demands and which clauses take the form of desired demands that are not necessarily vital. Though the latter are important, they cover those provisions that can be compromised in the design of implementable housing strategies.

Traditionally such briefs have been drawn up as a series of standards to be met by the designer. They not only stipulate *what* is to be provided but also *how* it is to be achieved. Such standards inevitably preclude any alternative ways of meeting the client's brief. For instance, a standard giving instructions for the location of schools might be written as: 'No dwelling should be further than 800 m from a primary school by a pedestrian route which does not cross a major road'. Such a brief, written as standard, excludes the possibility of any alternative to the location of primary schools at 1600 m centres throughout residential areas. On examining the intentions behind this instruction, it will be apparent that it has been designed to limit the travel time of children to school to 20 min and on the assumption that most children will walk to school, this has been expressed as the distance of 800 m. Recognition of the hazards of children crossing major traffic routes has also led to the stipulation that a main road is not allowed to intersect the route to school.

An alternative way of writing the clauses of a brief is to express them as performance specification. Performance specifications tell the designer what to do, or what performance is to be achieved but do not stipulate how to do it. In a client-oriented approach to housing where the briefs are derived directly from the actual demands of representatives of each client group, the reasons for each demand can also be incorporated in the performance specification clause. In this way, the designer is not only instructed what to do, but why he should do it, thus leaving all options open for design initiative and innovation. The standard given above expressed as a performance specification might read: 'No child should have to spend more than 20 min in travelling between home and a primary school, and his journey should be free of any danger from vehicular traffic'. Written in such a way, the designer is free to make any proposal as long as the performance is met. For instance pedestrian routes could cross major roads in underpasses or toy bridges; or a school bus system could be proposed allowing for a wider distribution of bigger schools still within 20 min travelling time. Performance specifications tend to be more complicated than simple rigid standards. Therefore it may be useful to append a 'deemed-to-satisfy' clause, which demonstrates one of the ways by which the performance can be met. The example of the standard concerning school location, given above, could be used as a deemed-to-satisfy clause to exemplify one way in which to meet the brief.

It may not be possible to express all clauses of the brief as flexible performance specifications at the same time as leaving no ambiguity as to what to do. There is little point in writing a brief in terms as vague as: 'All dwellings should have adequate access to public services.' It gives no instruction to the designer who has to implement the brief and a legal dispute over the subjective evaluation of what is 'adequate' would be a tortuous and unsatisfactory affair. In these cases rigid standards will have to be laid down. It is important, however, that all such standards should be reviewed frequently as a check on their continued applicability in a changing society and economy.

References

MOSER, C. A., *Survey Methods in Social Investigation*, Heinemann, London, 1961.
OPPENHEIM, A. N., *Questionnaire Design and Attitude Measurement*, Heinemann, London, 1968.
BURTON, T. L. and CHERRY, G. E., *Social Research Techniques for Planners*, George Allen and Unwin, London, 1970.
STACEY, M., *Method of Social Research*, Pergamon Press, London, 1970.
GARRETT, A., *Interviewing: Its Principles and Methods*, Family Service Association of America, New York, 1970.

STRATEGY PLANNING

An aid for the classification of courses of action by their 'levels and fields' of operation as required for the effective planning of urban housing strategies.

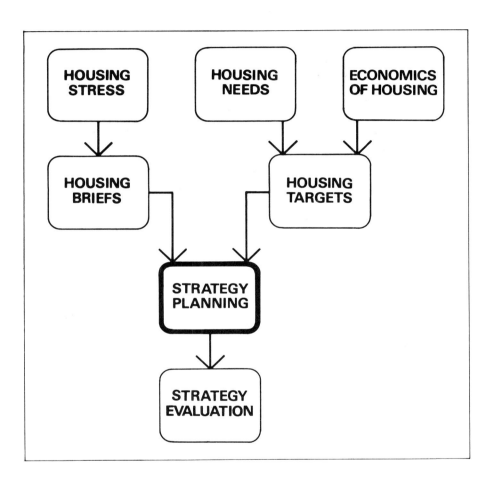

5

Once a problem has been identified alleviating it becomes the objective. The way to go about achieving an objective is called a strategy. The strategy objective states the principal, and usually the culminating action. For example, if the problem that had been identified was the 'lack of water', then the objective is to overcome this by the 'provision of water'. The next stage would then be to plan a strategy, or way of achieving this. Each strategy would be based on a different idea for supplying the water (collection from roof-tops, wells, extension of the existing piped-water system, reducing consumption, etc.). Each of the strategies would consist of a series of actions, from administrative to executive or operational measures (assessing the water requirements, authorization to go ahead with the project, financing to the laying of the pipes and the actual supply of water). The principal, and final action of each strategy would be the provision of water. The other actions, though essential, are means of achieving that objective.

Strategy planning consists of determining the whole series of actions that are required to meet the objectives of the strategy, determining who shall carry out each of those actions, how and in which order. The main problem is of course to make sure that *all* the requisite actions have been thought of. Once this has been ensured, then to allocate these jobs or roles to the relevant operators or actors is relatively easy. In order to meet any objective, there will be a number of ways of going about it, each based on a different idea, or concept, or group of ideas. Once each strategy has been planned, it will be necessary to select which one should be implemented.

In planning a new strategy, it will be found that a number of the roles or job-descriptions match those that existing institutions, organizations or individuals are already performing. In other cases, the existing actors might be found to be playing a role that is diametrically opposed to that required by the strategy. In the first case actors constitute a resource that the strategy can utilize. In the second case, the existing actors might be thought of as constraints that will have to be overcome if the strategy is to be successful. For example, at the District level, in the Legislative field, the Borough Council might have a Building Regulations Department to which all plans have to be submitted. It could be that in a strategy to provide water 'on tap', it was intended to collect rainwater off the roof of each house. Now, the Building Regulations Department, which is the actor concerned with obtaining legislative approval for the scheme, might have, as part of its existing role, a Regulation that stipulates (*inter alia*) ". . . all roofs are to have a pitch of not less than 40°". If this means that water collection is facilitated by such a roof design then this clause of the building regulation would be classified as a resource. On the other hand, another bye-law, based on an obsolete public health concern for the spread of malaria, might stipulate that ". . . all surface water is to be discharged directly to soak away or into the public drainage disposal system".

This regulation would have to be classified as a constraint and would demand action for the change of the bye-law in order to effect the particular strategy. Alternatively the collection system for rainwater could be modified to remain within the letter of the law, or the whole strategy would have to be reconsidered. There will also be situations where there is a gap in the existing structure and no actor exists that could perform a particular role, and in this case a new organization or institution would have to be created, or an existing institution could be expanded or supplemented to fit the bill. This, in itself, might mean initiating a further set of actions to help establish the required institution or organization.

Strategy planning, then, is the process of identifying the various jobs or actions that are needed to ensure that the objectives are met. Each of these jobs would then have to be matched against those in the existing structure to assess what resources there are and what constraints exist. In order to do this it is necessary to know what various organizations, institutions, bodies and individuals, actually do—what their role is. Often these institutions have names or titles that are not fully descriptive of their role, and indeed often an institution may act as an umbrella organization for a number of sub-institutions, with a wide range of operations. For example, a Social Welfare Department might have under it all sorts of sub-departments from those maintaining an employment register, to those distributing free milk to children. Some of these may be directly concerned with housing (rent subsidies) and others indirectly; or they could be made to make housing part of their concern; (e.g. 'employment' on self-help schemes instead of supplementary benefits), while others still may have nothing to do with housing.

In order to overcome this, and make sure that the right organization has been identified, both in planning a strategy and in comparing it to the existing framework, every actor must be identified by his role. This can be further clarified by classifying each role by both the field in which it operates, and by the level at which it operates. Field of operation means the area in which the actor is primarily operating, which in an urban-housing context would be one of the following: Political (including policy-making), Legislative (including legal), Financial, Administrative, Technical or Operational. Level means simply the level at which the actor operates from National (or even International), through Regional, Urban District, Community down to Household. The levels and fields of operations can be arranged in the form of a matrix, with the rows and columns acting as co-ordinates by which every actor can be classified (Fig. 2.29) Such a matrix is the basis for the Strategy Planning Chart, the Ideas Bank and the Resource Inventory, which together constitute a tool

Field of operation

Level of operation	Political	Legislative	Financial	Administrative	Technical	Executive
National regional						
Metropolitan						
District						
Community						
Household						

Fig. 2.29 Matrix of levels and fields of operation
Each element in the matrix is an organization, institution or individual whose role is identified by the level and field in which they operate.

for ensuring that any strategy is planned comprehensively and that it takes into account all the actions necessary for meeting the strategy objectives. It also helps to evaluate the existing institutions and to identify them as constraints, resources or non-existent *vis-à-vis* the proposed strategy. Whereas the Resources Inventory and the strategy planning charts are gridded both ways (levels as well as fields), the Ideas Bank is gridded by fields, but only graded by level from National to Household (Fig. 2.30).

The ideas bank

As the name suggests, the purpose of the Ideas Bank is to act as a depository for ideas that can be drawn upon as the need arises. Not all the alternatives deposited in the Ideas Bank will necessarily be used, nor of course, will concepts used in the Strategies be restricted to those in the Ideas Bank. Initially therefore, it is not important to have fully worked out or only feasible suggestions in the Ideas Bank. If an idea is thought to be useful, then it can be made workable later. What is important, however, is that there be a lot of ideas, however crazy, which can be drawn upon. The Ideas Bank can be filled up with options as and when they occur throughout the programme. Additionally, it is useful to have a Brain-storming session around the problems encountered by the Client groups, and to enter the resulting ideas in the Ideas Bank chart. It is sometimes difficult to establish where to locate a particular idea on the chart, since obviously each will have ramifications which will overspill to many other levels and fields. It helps, therefore, to restrict the entry to the one or two fields to which the idea is germane.

Resource inventory

This should classify every institution or organization or individual that is, or could be, a resource or a constraint to Housing in the broadest sense. Each of them should be entered by name in the relevant box. In some cases an organization will have several departments, which operate at different levels or in different fields. In this case, the name of the relevant department should be entered on to the Inventory. The Inventory chart should be based on a card or file index system which lists in more detail the operations of the various entries of the Inventory, together with addresses, names of contacts, etc.

Strategy planning

With the objective of meeting the Design Brief (which has been derived from the Client's Brief), go through the Ideas Bank, selecting all those ideas that might be even remotely useful. These can be entered on to a separate Ideas Bank for that particular Client group. Take any option at random from this new Ideas Bank, and call it A. Go through the Ideas Bank, annotating with the letter A all those concepts that could be compatible to A. Next, take another idea, and call it B, and annotate all those that are compatible with B. Repeat until each idea in the Bank has at least one letter allocated to it. Some ideas will be compatible to more ideas than others, while some will be compatible to all, and some to none. Each set of compatible alternatives can form the basis of a possible Strategy (Figs 2.30 and 2.31). Choose one set of ideas, and enter them on to the Strategy Planning Chart at the relevant level and field. This will be the chart for Strategy A, or it can be given a catch phrase that reflects the general drift of the ideas (Fig. 2.32).

Take one of the ideas entered in one of the boxes on the Strategy Planning Chart. See if there are any prerequisites for that idea to be im-

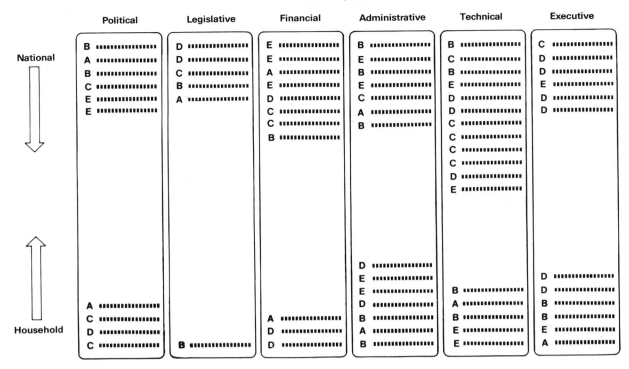

Fig. 2.30 Ideas Bank
Annotate comparable ideas with the same prefix. Transfer all ideas comparable to one concept on to its own Ideas Bank.

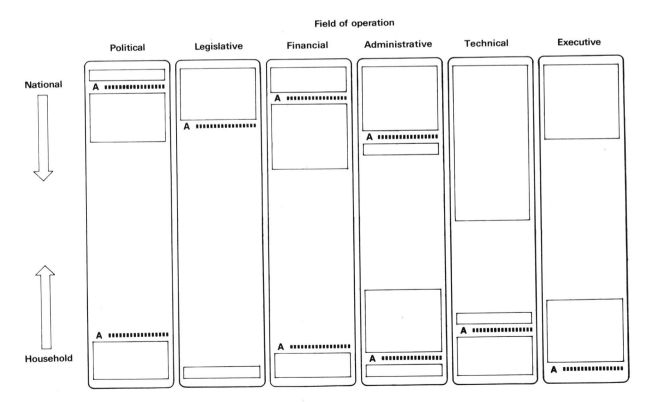

Fig. 2.31 Ideas Bank
Transfer all ideas comparable to one concept on to its own Ideas Bank.

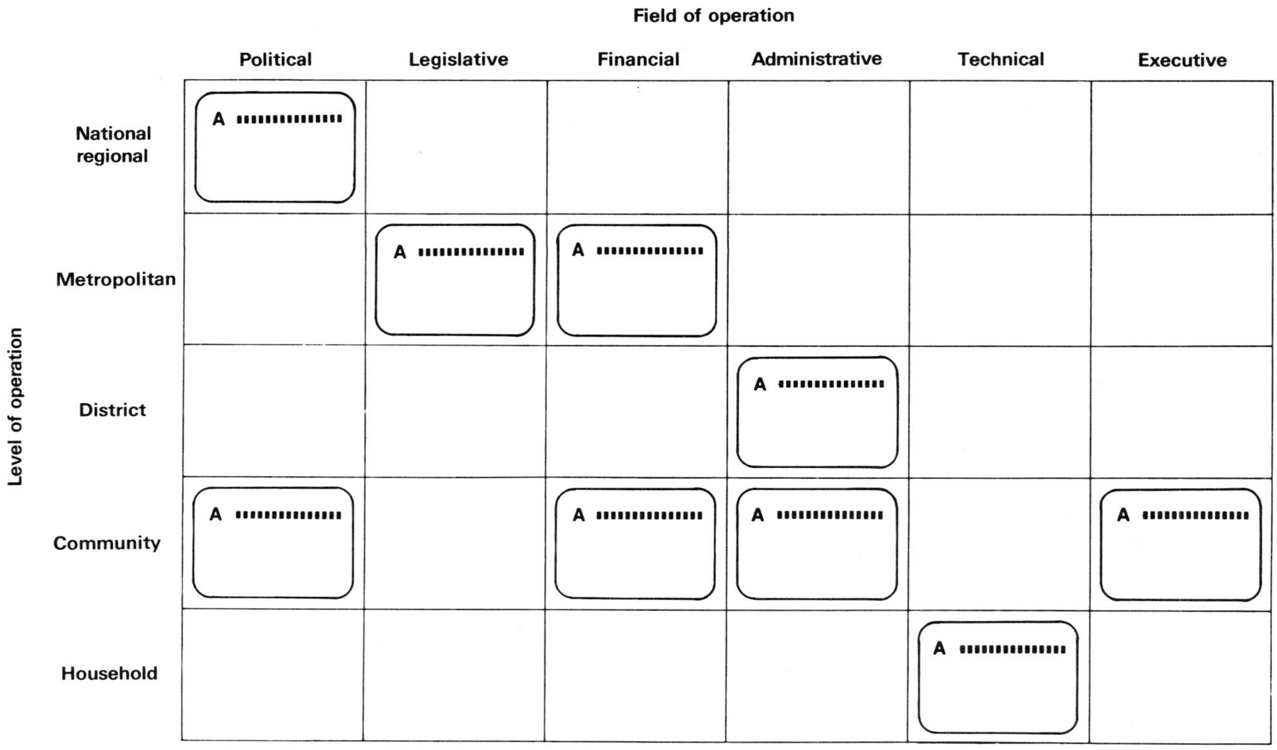

Fig. 2.32 Strategy planning chart
Transfer ideas on to Strategy planning chart at relevant level of operation.

plemented, if so, enter that in the relevant box. Say the idea was to collect rainwater from roofs. The prerequisite is to have the roof to be so designed. The prerequisite for that could be to assess whether there is sufficient rainfall in the area to make rainwater collection feasible, and if so what area of collector is required. Continue filling in prerequisites till either another idea-box is reached, or till the strategy planning stage is reached. Repeat for each idea.

Next fill in the consequences for each idea, including the consequences of the consequences, etc. until the Client's demands are met. Next connect up the boxes by arrows, starting from the action that needs to be taken first, numbering that 1, going on to the next action numbering that 2 and so on. There might well be two or more actions that occur simultaneously, in which case they will have the same number. In other instances, two or more actions are prerequisites for and thus lead to the next action. In this case there will be arrows from each of those action boxes to the subsequent action box.

Similarly arrows may go from a box to more than one other box if that action then leads to a number of other actions (Fig. 2.33). The next step is to see whether any box or even group of boxes have been left unconnected to the others. If this is so, it may be because there are in fact two or more strategies, or it could be that some steps have been left out. If it is the latter, fill in the missing steps. If it is the former, see whether the two strategies are separate, or whether one is a sub-strategy. In either case, it should have its own Planning chart. In fact every box of the strategy may have to have its own planning chart to show how it will be

Field of operation

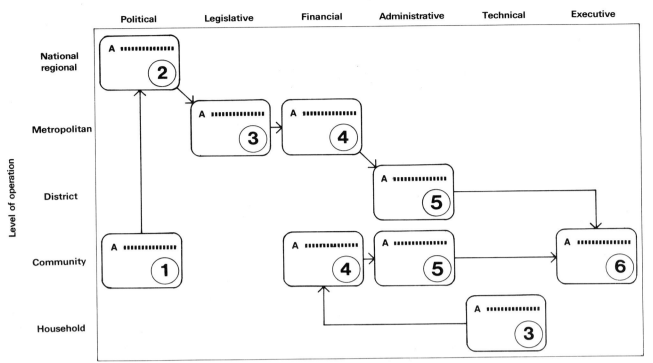

Fig. 2.33 **Strategy planning chart**
Fill in prerequisites and consequences, number boxes sequentially and link them with arrows.

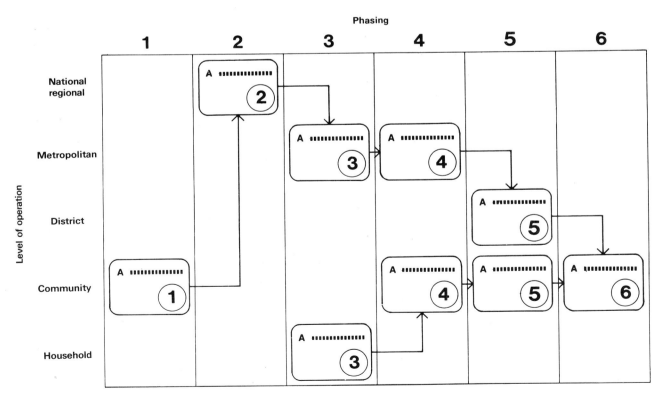

Fig. 2.34 **Strategy flow chart**
Box 3 at Household level has considerable float time and could be started any time between stages 1 and 3.

worked out. Now, take each box of the Strategy Planning Chart in turn and see whether the action specified in that box can be performed by the actor in the corresponding box of the Resource Inventory. Indicate whether the individual or institution is capable of playing the role specified for it, or whether it needs to be modified. In this case, or in the case where there is at present no actor, a new organization will have to be set up. This itself could lead to further additional actions on the Strategy Planning Chart. If this is so, consideration will have to be given to whether this additional set of actions may not be more difficult to achieve than altering the strategy such that that action is no longer necessary, say by bypassing or devising another way of doing it. The next step is to redraw the Strategy Planning Chart boxes in the form of a flow chart, such that the first box or boxes are those that were numbered 1 on the original chart (Fig. 2.34).

The numbers 1, 2 etc., are the stages necessary to implement the Strategy. By looking at the actions entailed in each stage, a time can be alloted to each stage. Thus an overall time-span for the achievement of the strategy objectives can be arrived at. It also becomes possible to define critical stages or actions without the completion of which the strategy will not progress, and those activities that have considerable 'float' time, and may even be bypassed. Each of the boxes specifies the brief for each action. The next stage would be to work out the details according to that brief.

The detailing might take the form of a set of drawings, reports, interviews, statements, accounts, etc. The sum total of all these would constitute the Strategy.

If a number of strategies were being worked out, it would be possible to plot them all on to one Strategy Planning Chart. It will become apparent that there are some strategies that have all their actions in the top left corner of the chart, and they would be the more general policy strategies; whereas those in the bottom right-hand section will be the more technical, localized strategies. In the majority of cases, however, there will be a considerable amount of overlap. Some of these will be actions requiring actors in parallel, or using different facets of the same actor or organization; but others will be similar if not identical in their role definition. It could be that the overlapping strategies are complementary, in that the same action would meet both objectives; or they could be in competition, where the meeting of one requirement would result in the failure to meet the requirements of another strategy. Such differences would need to be resolved at the Policy level. Indeed, the various decisions, roles and actors being created in the strategies, and the strategies themselves, will to a large extent determine the shape of a housing policy.

Example

Strategy for the Provision of Housing for the Future Low-Income Households.

This strategy was planned in the context of a socialist state, where the provision of housing for all citizens was already a stated policy objective. The central concept behind this strategy was to replace rents (which are based on size of dwellings) by a tax (which could be based on income),

Field of operation

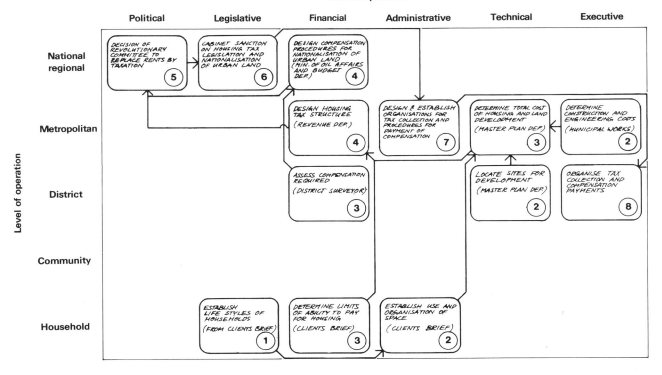

Fig. 2.35 Strategy planning chart

Field of operation

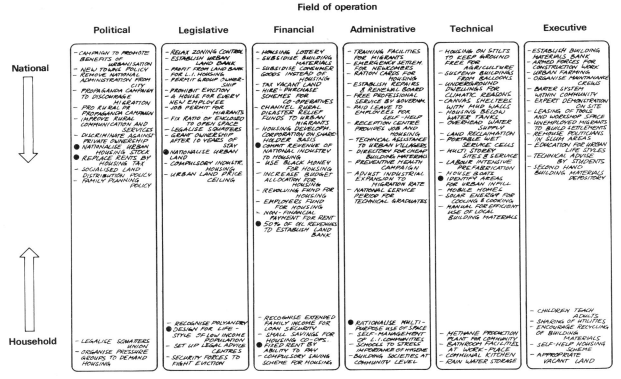

Fig. 2.36 Ideas Bank

Field of operation

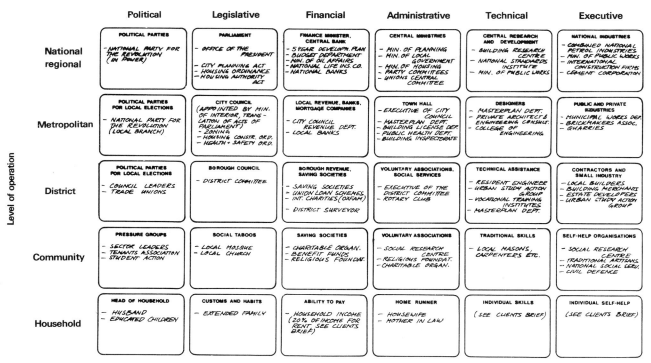

Level of operation	Political	Legislative	Financial	Administrative	Technical	Executive
National regional	**POLITICAL PARTIES** - NATIONAL PARTY FOR THE REVOLUTION (IN POWER)	**PARLIAMENT** - OFFICE OF THE PRESIDENT - CITY PLANNING ACT. - HOUSING ORDINANCE - HOUSING AUTHORITY ACT	**FINANCE MINISTER, CENTRAL BANK** - 5 YEAR DEVELOPM. PLAN - BUDGET DEPARTMENT - MIN. OF OIL AFFAIRS - NATIONAL LIFE INS. CO. - NATIONAL BANKS	**CENTRAL MINISTRIES** - MIN. OF PLANNING - MIN. OF LOCAL GOVERNMENT - MIN. OF HOUSING - PARTY COMMITTEES - UNIONS CENTRAL COMMITTEE	**CENTRAL RESEARCH AND DEVELOPMENT** - BUILDING RESEARCH CENTRE - NATIONAL STANDARDS INSTITUTE - MIN. OF PUBLIC WORKS	**NATIONAL INDUSTRIES** - COMBINED NATIONAL PETROL INDUSTRIES - MIN. OF PUBLIC WORKS - INTERNATIONAL CONSTRUCTION FIRMS - CEMENT CORPORATION
Metropolitan	**POLITICAL PARTIES FOR LOCAL ELECTIONS** - NATIONAL PARTY FOR THE REVOLUTION (LOCAL BRANCH)	**CITY COUNCIL** (APPOINTED BY MIN. OF INTERIOR, TRANS-LATION OF ACTS OF PARLIAMENT) - ZONING - HOUSING CONSTR. ORD. - HEALTH + SAFETY ORD.	**LOCAL REVENUE, BANKS, MORTGAGE COMPANIES** - CITY COUNCIL REVENUE DEPT. - LOCAL BANKS	**TOWN HALL** - EXECUTIVE OF CITY COUNCIL - MASTERPLAN DEPT. - BUILDING LICENSE DEP. - PUBLIC HEALTH DEPT. - BUILDING INSPECTORATE	**DESIGNERS** - MASTERPLAN DEPT. - PRIVATE ARCHITECT & ENGINEERING CONSULT. - COLLEGE OF ENGINEERING	**PUBLIC AND PRIVATE INDUSTRIES** - MUNICIPAL WORKS DEP. - BRICKMAKERS ASSOC. - QUARRIES
District	**POLITICAL PARTIES FOR LOCAL ELECTIONS** - COUNCIL LEADERS - TRADE UNIONS	**BOROUGH COUNCIL** - DISTRICT COMMITTEE	**BOROUGH REVENUE, SAVING SOCIETIES** - SAVING SOCIETIES - UNION LOAN SCHEMES - INT. CHARITIES (OXFAM) - DISTRICT SURVEYOR	**VOLUNTARY ASSOCIATIONS, SOCIAL SERVICES** - EXECUTIVE OF THE DISTRICT COMMITTEE - ROTARY CLUB	**TECHNICAL ASSISTANCE** - RESIDENT ENGINEER - URBAN STUDY ACTION GROUP - VOCATIONAL TRAINING INSTITUTES - MASTERPLAN DEPT.	**CONTRACTORS AND SMALL INDUSTRY** - LOCAL BUILDERS - BUILDING MERCHANTS - ESTATE DEVELOPERS - URBAN STUDY ACTION GROUP
Community	**PRESSURE GROUPS** - SECTOR LEADERS - TENANTS ASSOCIATION - STUDENT ACTION	**SOCIAL TABOOS** - LOCAL MOSQUE - LOCAL CHURCH	**SAVING SOCIETIES** - CHARITABLE ORGAN. - BENEFIT FUNDS - RELIGIOUS FOUNDAT.	**VOLUNTARY ASSOCIATIONS** - SOCIAL RESEARCH CENTRE - RELIGIOUS FOUNDAT. - CHARITABLE ORGAN.	**TRADITIONAL SKILLS** - LOCAL MASONS, CARPENTERS ETC.	**SELF-HELP ORGANISATIONS** - SOCIAL RESEARCH CENTRE - TRADITIONAL ARTISANS - NATIONAL SOCIAL SERV. - CIVIL DEFENCE
Household	**HEAD OF HOUSEHOLD** - HUSBAND - EDUCATED CHILDREN	**CUSTOMS AND HABITS** - EXTENDED FAMILY	**ABILITY TO PAY** - HOUSEHOLD INCOME (20% OF INCOME FOR RENT, SEE CLIENTS BRIEF)	**HOME RUNNER** - HOUSEWIFE - MOTHER IN LAW	**INDIVIDUAL SKILLS** (SEE CLIENTS BRIEF)	**INDIVIDUAL SELF-HELP** (SEE CLIENTS BRIEF)

Fig. 2.37 Resource Inventory

whereby housing could be provided that was of the size required by the household, not merely that which it could afford. This led to determining what the cost involved would be, both in terms of compensation to be paid for nationalizing existing housing stock and land, and for production of new houses. The latter led to the need for an investigation of the size and type of housing required in order to arrive at its costs. The strategy is shown on the Strategy Planning Chart (Fig. 2.35). The Ideas Bank and Resource Inventory for it is shown in Figs 2.36 and 2.37 respectively.

STRATEGY EVALUATION

A technique for the selection of criteria for the evaluation of alternative courses of action.

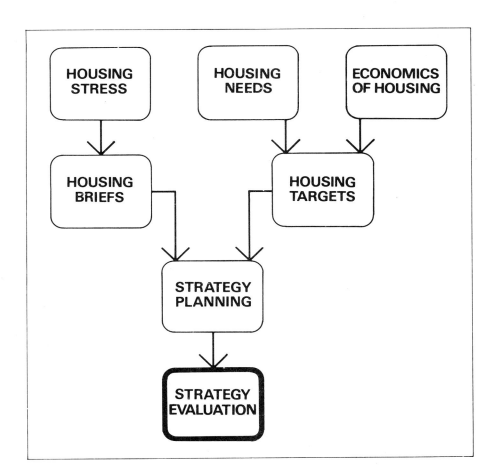

6

The Design Brief acts as a check-list against which a strategy can be tested. Obviously a strategy that does not meet the design brief does not meet the Client's demands, and would be rejected in a client-oriented housing programme.

Testing whether a strategy does or does not meet a set of previously laid down objectives, is a fundamental evaluation technique. To evaluate means 'to determine value'. Unfortunately 'value' is not an objective quality, nor is it absolute. It is relative and subjective; any process of evaluation has to overcome this, as far as possible, by externalizing and making transparent the value-judgements involved.

All decisions to do something, or indeed not to do something, are the result of evaluating alternatives. Each course of action or inaction will entail expending resources (time, energy, money) as the result of which there will accrue certain advantages. In theory action will be taken whenever advantages outweigh expenditure. In practice, there is considerable inertia which has to be overcome before people or institutions will embark on a new course of action. This inertia is caused by fear of the untested and untried and by a hesitancy to relinquish the known and existing situation to which one has become accustomed. Therefore in practice, the surplus of advantages over cost has to exceed a certain minimum before a course of action will be embarked upon.

Where both the input and the outcome are in the same unit (of time or money or effort), comparison, and calculations of surplus are straightforward, and evaluation is relatively simple. However as this is seldom the case, the first step is usually to convert one or the other of the inputs or outputs into units that can be compared. This means assigning values.

Let us say that I decide to buy a balloon for one penny 'because I like it'. In this case there were three courses of action open to me. (1) To buy the balloon; (2) To buy something else; and (3) To buy nothing. By opting for the first course, I am putting a certain value on the pleasure that I derive from possessing a balloon, and to me at that time, the value of that pleasure is higher than one penny, and higher than the value of anything else I could have bought instead. One does not always go through such an evaluation process consciously but usually acts when one considers one is getting 'good value'. In the above example a personal scale of values was being applied, and the evaluation was totally subjective and personal, thus, the decision is not open to dispute. However, when making decisions for other people an explicit scale of values is needed.

In a market economy, the scale of values is given by the money-value of commodities (including time), and there is an implicit assumption that every commodity can have a monetary value attached to it, and that the market forces of supply and demand operate to ensure that a fair and universally acceptable price is arrived at. The criterion of 'profit maximization' is then used to evaluate alternatives. Under welfare economics, the objective would be to maximize welfare. A preferred course of action would be that which 'left at least one member of society better off than before without making any other member of society any worse off than before'.

We have seen the need for attaching values in order to convert to units of the same denomination. There is also the need to be able to compare values that accrue or are expended at different times. Not only is the value of one pound sterling now different to that of a pound five years ago, but so is the value of having a balloon now different to having one in five years time. Generally speaking it is preferable to have something now rather than later. In order to be able to equate values over time, devices such as rates of interest and discounting have been developed. Money can be discounted over time (that is, calculating the present value of a future sum of money), by using the rate of interest prevalent in the market. The rate of interest can be said to fluctuate to reflect the opportunity cost of capital.

Opportunity cost is the cost in terms of the values of alternatives or of other opportunities that have to be foregone to achieve a particular end. However, instead of using the market rate of interest, one might think in terms of using a rate of discounting that reflects the value that society puts on consumption now versus consumption in the future. This is called the 'social rate of time preference'.

The other important point is 'goal definition'. In a client-oriented approach, the goal is to meet the clients' demands, and strategies can be evaluated by the degree to which they meet these.

However, there might well be other objectives to meet, over and above the Clients' demands. It is important that all of these are fully articulated before an evaluation can be attempted. For example, in selecting alternative sites for a housing project, a site on the southern edge of a town may be chosen in preference to one on the north, because the costs are marginally less. However, if one were to take into account the additional goals of the Town Council (not of the Clients), to expand the town generally northwards, this might reverse the siting preference. Sometimes the planner or designer has to satisfy more than one Client group. Their demands may be such that conflicting goals have to be met. In such cases, it is necessary to weight or rank goals. It could be that a simple split into essential and desirable goals will suffice to resolve the issue. However more sophisticated variants of this situation may occur and make it necessary to weight the goals or objectives of one Client group against another. This might be done according to the size of Client group to achieve a majority verdict, or the weighting might be reversed to protect a minority view.

Over the years, a number of evaluation techniques for planners have been developed, from economic theory. Some of these may be used at various stages of strategy development with appropriate modifications.

The main stumbling blocks in any evaluation technique are:

Evaluation chart

(1) Choice of criteria, or *Goal Definition*.
(2) Whether or not values are constant or should they be corrected by *Weighting*.
(3) How the evaluator can maintain his *Objectivity*.
(4) How to attach *Values*, particularly to *Intangibles*.

The Evaluation Chart is a tool that has been devised to allow decisions to be taken about choosing an alternative in such a way that the decision-maker is fully aware of the ramifications implicit and explicit in his decision.

Basically it is a matrix whose columns are the different alternatives being assessed and whose rows are the different groups being affected by them. The value at the intersection is the cost or benefit accruing to that particular group by that particular proposal. All values are entered in the denomination in which they occur, or can be converted to an index or percentage, but cannot be summed vertically by columns. They can only be compared horizontally in rows. Obviously therefore, no single figure,

103

giving the overall cost or benefit will emerge. The evaluation chart is a tool that makes it possible for a decision to be made by the decision-makers, not a substitute for them.

Method

Once the feasible alternatives that meet the clients' briefs have been worked out, a list of all the groups of people and organizations that will be effected by them should be drawn up, starting with the Client groups. Each of these groups should then be assigned to a row, both in the costs and in the benefits half of the evaluation chart, even though some groups may not incur both. A final grouping of 'The Rest' should also be included to account for externalities. Most, if not all, of these groups will have been identified in the Strategy Planning Chart for each strategy.

Each of the columns should then be headed by the title of a strategy that is being evaluated. It might be interesting and sometimes even necessary, to record the costs and benefits of not implementing any of the strategies, and allowing the existing situation to continue, in which case, the first column would be headed 'laissez-faire'.

The value of the cost incurred, or benefit accruing to each group as a consequence of each alternative, should then be entered at the relevant intersection. The details of how this value has been arrived at should be indicated in a set of Notes. Where a numerical value is known or can be calculated, as a monetary figure or number of people housed etc., this should be entered either as that value, or it can be converted to a percent figure related to a known value. Where the value is not numerical, or is an intangible, the relative cost or benefit along a row should be indicated and again, amplified in the Notes. For example, if strategy A is siting people such that they have access to three bus routes, strategy B to one and strategy C to two, then the values along the row might read as High, Low, Medium, respectively, with the notes explaining why these values have been allocated.

It will be appreciated that the chart is a form of double entry account, and therefore each time one group incurs a cost, another group must be receiving it as a benefit. Where this other group is external, or peripheral, the benefit can be added to the account of 'The Rest', and explained in the Notes.

For most purposes it will be necessary to assess costs and benefits over a period of time, say 20 years, and it is important that all values are discounted over the same time period. It might also be useful to differentiate between short and long term costs, and this can be done by subdividing the columns for each alternative strategy into 'initial columns' (for the first year) and 'eventual columns' (for the remaining years).

Once the chart has been completed, it can be used to help decide which strategy to select. In a client-oriented approach, obviously the main criteria, or goals will be to maximize benefits and minimize costs for the client group. To this end, it is important that any intangible values entered along the clients' rows are derived from information gathered during Survey, and incorporated in the Clients' Brief. In other words, it should not reflect the evaluators' subjective values, but rather the clients'.

If there is only one client group, then by reading along the row for that group, the relative costs and benefits can be read off for the different strategies, and the most cost-effective, taking both tangibles and intangibles into account, can be selected. The other values, while not being for purposes of selection, will still be needed in order to assess what the costs and benefits to other groups will be, as a consequence of selecting that strategy.

It is possible that despite having selected a strategy that is most apt for the client group, the resources required to implement it are just not there. This makes it unavoidable to choose the next best strategy for the client that can be implemented.

In case there is more than one client group, or there are sub-groups, the selection procedure would involve looking at the implications for all of them. If they agree on the strategy which gives them the better value, there is obviously no problem in selecting that strategy. However, when there is no strategy that is best for all, and there might even be contradictory recommendations, then it will be necessary to employ some form of weighting to choose a strategy. This weighting can either reflect the relative sizes of the groups or respond to some other (external) goal such as promoting one group over another. This basic model can obviously be altered to suit other evaluation purposes, which may or may not be client-oriented.

A large site fairly close to the city centre was bought by the City Council for development as middle income housing. Some way through the programme, the Council ran out of funds, and suspended operations. Completed houses were sold off to individual buyers, but after a few years the rest of the site was taken over by squatters. Later the Council decided to revive the scheme, partly because its finances had improved, but largely as part of a 'slum clearance drive'. The squatters, though detested by the middle income residents, wielded too much political power to be ousted, and the Council was looking for the 'best' way of housing them 'properly' on the site.

Example

Two alternative proposals were worked out. These are presented below for evaluation, along with the consequences of doing nothing. The two proposals differ only in as much as one is for a 'site and services scheme', and the other for the provision of completed housing units. In other respects, such as layout and the provision of space, services and amenities, the two schemes are virtually identical. The evaluation itself is done for the following three cases:

Case 1: Client group: Low-income tenants
Case 2: Client group: Existing squatters
Case 3: Client group: Existing squatters and low-income tenants.

Choosing a strategy

Case 1: Client group:
low-income tenants

In this instance, both the proposed alternatives are clearly preferable to continuing the existing situation. From a short-term point of view, the monetary costs of completed houses seem far higher than site and services but when considering the benefits, the priorities are reversed. In fact, the Notes reveal that because this Client group has families and is in full-time occupation, it would want to build the dwellings on the serviced sites sooner rather than later. This would have the effect for most of them of bringing the 'long term' costs into the short term. In other words, whereas the costs are represented as short (1 year) and long (19 years) term, in this case, all the costs would be incurred within the next 2 years for the site and services strategy. Whereas for the completed houses strategy they would be spread over the next 20 years. Therefore, since the overall costs are lower and benefits higher, the completed houses strategy should be chosen.

Case 2: Client group: existing squatters

The argument presented in Case 1 also applies for this group, except that for site and services, the costs mentioned under 'long term' are more likely to be spread over a long time, and a lot of the costs are likely to be on paper, since lack of employment in this group is more likely to lead to self-help building. In this case, the site and services strategy might be selected.

Case 3: Client groups: existing squatters and low-income tenants

From the arguments above, it will be apparent that the choice of the strategy depends on what weight one attaches to each of the client groups.

However, if we look at the Notes, we find that the Government is keen to encourage middle-scale contractors. This might be a reason for the Government to subsidize the completed houses as a means of stimulation of the building industry. Such a subsidy, or even a Government directive to that effect might be decisive in recommending the completed houses alternative.

(1) Low-income Tenants (Mostly of squatter 'landlords'. Migrants from villages, large families).

(2) Existing Squatter Households (Moved into area when City Council stopped building on site. Mainly bachelor households).

(3) City Council (City's administrative organization. Elected. Owns part of the land).

(4) City Housing Authority (Recently set up to manage City Council housing, past as well as future).

(5) C.H.A. Admin. Dept (Handles allocation of Housing, Building and Planning legislation, Rents).

(6) C.H.A. Building Dept (Executes City Council housing and building work. Maintenance).

(7) City Rating Office (Sets and collects rates).

(8) City Treasurer (Pays for City services: Parks, Police, Schools).

(9) City Health Dept (Responsible for City Cleaning, Clinics).

(10) Ministry of Water and Power (Supply and installation).

(11) Squatter Landlords (Some of the earliest squatters, sub-letting rooms to families. Some building purely for rent).

(12) Surrounding Middle-income Residents (Owner-occupiers who bought the first Council houses. Some of them subsequently sold for a profit. Object to squatters lowering the 'tone of the area').

(13) Small-scale Contractors ('One man and a barrow'. Mostly learned trade by working on a building site for a year or two. No overheads, but also no credit facilities).

(14) Middle-scale Contractors (Local firms, being encouraged by Government to expand, given financial and management assistance).

(15) Material Suppliers (Hardware merchants with Limited stocks. Prefer cash-down payments).

Costs	Laissez-faire A	Sites & Services		Completed Houses	
		Short term B	Long term C	Short term D	Long term E
(1) Low-income tenants	High 2,844,000	Medium 45,504	High 1,798,830	Low 91,008	Low 1,729,152
(2) Existing squatters	High 915,600	Low 146,496	High 5648	Medium 292,992	Low 5,566,848
(3) City Council	1,200,000	200,000	—	200,000	—
(4) City Housing Authority	High	2,400,000	—	4,800,000	—
(5) C.H.A. administration	High	Some	High	Some	Some
(6) C.H.A. building	—	900,000	—	900,000	—
(7) City Rating Office	200,000	1000	9500	1500	9500
(8) City Treasurer	100,000	3000	57,000	3000	57,000
(9) City Health Department	100,000	2600	50,000	2600	50,000
(10) Ministry of Water & Power	480,000	524,000	456,000	524,000	456,000
(11) Squatter landlords	398,760	12,292	2,323,548	12,292	2,323,548
(12) Middle-income residents	High	Medium	Low	Low	Low
(13) Small-scale contractors	319,000	—	800,000	—	—
(14) Middle-scale contractors	—	1,280,000	—	896,000	—
(15) Material suppliers	—	192,000	1,200,000	1,344,000	—
(16) The Rest	Some	Some	—	Some	—

Evaluation chart

Benefits	Laissez-faire A	Sites & Services		Completed Houses	
		Short term B	Long term C	Short term D	Long term E
(17) Low-income tenants	Low	Low	Med-High	High	High
(18) Existing squatters	Medium	Medium	Med-High	High	High
(19) City Council	— ·	Medium	High 1,800,000	High	High 1,000,000
(20) City Housing Authority	— ·	Medium	Med-High	High	High
(21) C.H.A. administration	— ·	Low	Low	High	High
(22) C.H.A. Building	0	900,000	—	900,000	
(23) City Rating Office	— ·	1000	19,000	1000	19,000
(24) City Treasurer	— ·	4000	76,000	4000	76,000
(25) City Health Department	— ·	4000	76,000	4000	76,000
(26) Ministry of Water & Power	— ·	524,000	456,000	524,000	456,000
(27) Squatter landlords	22,445,840	237,000	—	237,000	—
(28) Middle-income residents	Low	Low	Medium	High	High
(29) Small-scale contractors	398,760	—	1,000,000	—	Some
(30) Middle-scale contractors	Some	460,000	—	1,120,000	—
(31) Material suppliers	— ·	240,000	1,500,000	1,680,000	Some
(32) The Rest	— ·		Some		Some

(1) A. High: Insecurity, harassment, overcrowding.
2,844,000 = 20 years' monthly rent.

B. Medium: Cheap housing, but core insufficient to meet immediate housing needs and therefore require immediate building of additions, or severe overcrowding.

C. High: Cost of building operations involved in making additions to cores. Unlikely to get loans except from money-lenders at exorbitant interest rates. Probably need building immediately.
1,798,830 = cost of additions.

D. Low: Higher cost of repayments compensated by ability to move immediately into finished houses.
91,008 = 1 year's repayments.

E. Low: Convenience of having properly built houses with low maintenance costs.
1,729,152 = 19 years' repayments.

(2) A. High: Insecurity, harassment, overcrowding.
915,600 = 20 years' 'rent' (protection money).

B. Low: Cheap housing. Size of core-house sufficient for present needs of households.
146,496 = 1 year's repayments.

C. High: Lower repayments offset by need to borrow from money-lenders and build using individual contractors.
5,648,424 = cost of building additions.

D. Medium: High repayments offset by convenience of completed houses ready for occupation and possibility of calling in rural members of household who help supplement income.
292,992 = 1 year's repayments.

E. Low: As above, completed with low maintenance costs.

(3) A. 1,200,000 = loss of earnings due to inability to sell off land being squatted on.

B. 200,000 = cost of subsidy of selling land at price lower than market rate.

D. As above.

(4) A. High: Political pressures to do something about squatting.

B. 2,400,000 = capital outlay for building core houses.

D. 4,800,000 = capital outlay for building housing units.

(5) A. High:

B. Some: Problems of allocations of housing units.

C. High: Problems of enforcing building regulations viz. additions, rent collections.

D. Some: Problems of allocation of housing units. Rent collections.

E. Some: Rent collection.

(6) B. 900,000 = designing costs.

D. 900,000 = designing costs.

(7) A. 200,000 = loss of rates.

B.	1000 = rates for one year.	
C.	9500 = rates for 19 years.	
D.	1000 = rates for 1 year.	
E.	9500 = rates for 19 years.	

(8) A.   1,000,000 = Abnormally high costs over average, for provision of schools and parks etc.

      B, D.   3000 = costs of providing services for 1 year.

      C, E.   57,000 = costs of providing services for 19 years.

(9) A.   100,000 = extra costs for provision of health services including pest control and other preventive measures and innoculations.

      B, D.   2600 = cost of health services for 1 year.

      C, E.   50,000 = cost of health services for 19 years.

(10) A.   480,000 = loss of earnings due to non-payments and 'stolen' electricity.

      B, D.   524,000 = cost of electricity and water supply.

      C, E.   456,000 = cost of electricity and water supply.

(11) A.   398,760 = payments to 'protection' squads for rent collection.

      B, D.   12,292 = loss of earnings for 1 year.

      C, e.   2,323,548 = loss of earnings for 19 years.

(12) A. High: Drop in property values, inconvenience, noise, nuisance.

      B. Medium: Betterment in surroundings, but still some element of temporary settlement and resultant nuisance.

      C, D, E. } Low: Improvement of locality, but still low income neighbours.

(13) A.   319,000 = cost of construction work in maintenance.

      C.   800,000 = cost of construction work on additions.

(14) B.   1,280,000 = cost of executing construction work of core houses.

      D.   896,000 = cost of executing construction work of housing units.

(15) B.   192,000 = cost of materials.

      C.   1,200,000 = cost of materials.

      D.   1,344,000 = cost of materials.

(16) A.   Some = subsidies to middle-scale contractors.

      B, D.   Some = utilization of funds to build housing deprives others from having possible use of them.

(17) A.   Low = low standard of housing provided.

      B.   Low = core houses too small for household needs.

      C.   Medium–High = additions by local builder, standard low.

      D, E.   High = instant amenity, high standard of construction.

(18) A.   Medium = low standard of amenity and space, but adequate for 'bachelors'.

	B.	Medium = core houses just large enough for immediate needs.
	C.	Medium–High = additions not completely satisfactory.
	D, E.	High = instant amenity, high standard of construction.
(19)	B.	Medium = some kudos as a consequence of having done something about the squatters—but this is lessened with core-houses.
	C, E.	High = as above, but without the lessening effect of core-houses.
		1,000,000 = income from sale of land.
(20)	B.	Medium = kudos for achieving objectives, but core-housing still reminiscent of temporary shelter.
	C.	Medium–High = additional kudos when additions completed to core-houses.
	D, E.	High = to outside world, completed houses give prestige to the C.H.A.
(21)	B, C.	Low.
	D, E.	High.
(22)	B, D.	900,000 = design fees.
(23)	B, D.	100 = share of rates allotted to rating office for 1 year.
	C, E.	19,000 = share of rates allotted to rating office for 19 years.
(24)	B, D.	4000 = share of rates to Treasury for 1 year.
	C, E.	76,000 = share of rates to Treasury for 19 years.
(25)	B, D.	4000 = share of rates allotted to City Health Department.
	C, E.	76,000 = share of rates allotted to Health.
(26)	B, D.	500,000 = connection charges + 24,000 = payment of bills.
A.		2,445,840 = rent collected.
	B, D.	237,000 = compensation paid upon compulsory purchase.
(28)	A.	
		Low = supply of cheap labour.
	B.	Low = core houses present a slightly better environment that squatter housing.
	C, E.	456,000 = payment of bills.
	C.	Medium = additions to cores make the site 'slum-like'.
	D, E.	High = houses built by C.H.A. create pleasant environment.
(29)	A.	398,760 = earnings from maintenance work carried out.
	C.	1,000,000 = earnings from building additions to core-houses.
	E.	Some = maintenance and additions.
(30)	A.	Some = Government subsidies.
	B.	160,000 = payment for construction of core-housing.

	D.	1,120,000 = payment for construction of housing units.
(31)	B.	240,000 = payment for materials supplied.
	C.	1,500,000 = payment for materials supplied.
	D.	1,680,000 = payment for materials supplied.
	E.	Some = payment for materials supplied.
(32)	C, D.	Some = return of capital to City can be used for other purposes.

References

HILL, M., A goals-achievement matrix in evaluation alternative plans, *Journal of the American Institute of Planning*, Vol. 34, Part 2, 1968.

KITCHING, L. C., Regional planning considerations, in Cambridgeshire et al, *Commission on the Third London Airport*, Evidence Submitted at Stage III, chapter 2, 1969.

KOZLOWSKI, J., Threshold theory and the sub-regional plan, *Town Planning Review*, Vol. 39, pp. 99–116, 1968.

KREDITOR, A., The provisional plan, *Industrial Development and the Development Plan*, chapter 8, Au Foras Forbartha, Dublin, 1967.

LEAN, W. & GOODALL, B., Aspects of Land Economics, *Estates Gazette*, London.

LICHFIELD, N., Cost-benefit analysis in urban expansion: A case study, Peterborough, *Regional Studies* 3, pp. 123–155, 1969.

LICHFIELD, N. and WENDT, P. F., Six English new towns: a financial appraisal, *Town Planning Review*, Vol. 40, pp. 284–314, 1969.

MACE, R., *Municipal Cost-Revenue Research in the United States*, The Institute of Government, The University of North Carolina.

MALISZ, B., Urban planning theory methods and results, in *City and Regional Planning in Poland*, (Ed., Fisher, J. C.), Cornell University Press, Ithaca, N.Y., 1966.

SCHLAGER, K., The Rank Based Expected Value Method of Plan Evaluation, Highway Research Record, No. 238, Highway Research Board, Washington D.C. The description is quoted from Boyce, E. and Day, N. D. (1969) *Metropolitan Plan Evaluation Methodology*, pp. 45–47, Institute for Environmental Studies, University of Pennsylvania.

STONE, P. A., Housing, Town Development, Land and Costs, *Estates Gazette*, London.

INDEX